Contents

LEADING STRATEGIC CHANGE, INNOVATION & TRANSFORMATION

The 10 Elements of Successful Change Leadership

For permission requests,
write to the author at the address below.
Leadership Alive, Inc. | PO Box 69652 | Tucson, AZ 85737

ISBN: 979-8-9886661-5-8 (paperback)
ISBN: 979-8-9887643-3-5 (hardback)
ISBN: 978-1-64316-179-2 (ebook)

LeadershipAlive.com
Chris@LeadershipAlive.com

Printed in the United States of America
Author: Christopher P. Meade, PhD
Cover design by Kevin Piazza
Editing team: David Elmore and Rob Peace

Dedication

This book is dedicated to the women and men who were part of the George Fox University MBA program, where I had the honor and privilege to teach the Organizational Change and Agility leadership course. Thank you for all that you taught me in our journey of learning together. I cherish many memories of you all.

Introduction

In the chessboard of business, change is the only
constant move, adaptability is the strategy, and
leaders are the grandmasters setting the pace.
— Christopher Meade, PhD

The Undeniable Necessity of Change

In today's fast-paced world, change is the name of the game. Companies face a relentless barrage of technological advancements, shifting consumer preferences, and disruptive forces that make standing still a one-way ticket to obsolescence. Like a chameleon adapting its colors to blend into the environment, businesses must continually transform themselves to remain relevant and competitive in the flux.

Picture yourself on a roller coaster, gripping the safety bar with white-knuckled anticipation as you career through the twists and turns. In the modern business landscape, if you're not braced for the wild ride and ready to adapt at a moment's notice, you might find yourself hurtling off the tracks.

The digital revolution has ushered in an era where being rendered obsolete lurks around every corner—like a shadowy figure in a horror movie, ready to pounce. Industries that once seemed impervious to change have been toppled by nimble upstarts harnessing the power of innovation. Take the once-mighty Blockbuster that was brought to its knees by Netflix, or the stalwart taxi industry gasping for air in the dominant wake of rideshare giants Uber and Lyft.

The message is clear: adapt or perish. In this tumultuous environment, change isn't a luxury. It's a necessity—the *sine qua non* of survival. To stay afloat in the stormy seas of business, leaders need to not only accept the inevitability of change but wholeheartedly embrace it.

The Critical Role of Transformative Leaders

But, as we know all too well, enacting change is easier said than done. Like steering a mammoth cruise ship through a narrow strait, navigating transformation requires skill, determination, and a steady hand at the helm. That's where leaders come in.

Effective leaders are more than just figureheads who bask in the limelight or deliver rousing speeches. They're the architects of change, the master conductors who orchestrate the complex symphony of transformation. They rally the troops, igniting the spark of innovation and steering the ship through the treacherous waters of the unknown.

It's no secret that change can be a tough pill to swallow. It's unsettling and uncomfortable, and it's met with resistance from those who cling to the familiar. But a great leader knows how to break through the barriers of inertia and fear, tapping into the boundless potential that lies within every organization.

In the words of the late Austrian-American consultant Peter Drucker, "The greatest danger in times of turbulence is not the turbulence; it is to act with yesterday's logic." The leaders who rise to the challenge of change are the ones who recognize that the rules of the game have not only shifted but become even more complex.

And great leaders are *not* afraid to rewrite the playbook.

10 Crucial Elements of Change Leaders

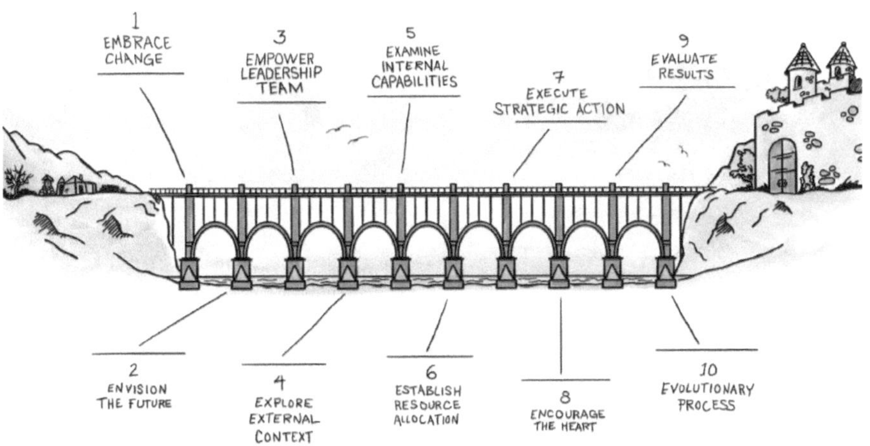

Have you ever felt like you were standing on one side of a canyon, with the future you envision unreachable on the other side of a broad chasm? I'm willing to wager that you have—and you're possibly even feeling that way right now. But with the right principles and strategy, you can build a bridge across that canyon and reach your new future. Through extensive research, we've identified the ten vital elements of successful change leadership, which form a powerful framework that equips leaders with the tools, insights, and strategies they need to thrive in the face of change.

Leading strategic change can feel like crossing that chasm that separates your team or organization from your goals. The challenge is building the firm but flexible bridge, which requires careful planning, vision, and execution. Think of these elements as the building blocks of change-driven leadership—they're the DNA that gives rise to an unstoppable force for transformation.

These elements work together, harmoniously propelling organizations on their journey toward a brighter and more innovative future. They help leaders emerge stronger, more adaptable, and ready to tackle whatever challenges the future holds. Below, let's take a look at the 10 Elements of Successful Change Leadership.

1. **Embrace Change:** cultivating a growth mindset
2. **Envision the Future:** charting a bold course
3. **Empower Your Leadership Team:** assembling a cohesive force
4. **Explore External Context:** deciphering the business landscape
5. **Examine Internal Capabilities:** unearthing hidden potential
6. **Establish Resource Allocation:** fueling the engine of change
7. **Execute Strategic Action:** translating vision into action
8. **Encourage the Heart:** igniting passion and commitment
9. **Evaluate the Results:** assessing the impact of change
10. **Evolutionary Process:** sustaining change and momentum

Let's dive into these elements and explore them further.

1. **Embrace Change.** The first step on the road to change leadership is embracing the inevitability of change itself. By cultivating a growth mindset and fostering a culture that views change as an opportunity rather than a threat, leaders can unleash the full potential of their teams and organizations.

2. **Envision the Future.** Great change leaders have a clear, compelling vision of the future—a destination that inspires and motivates their teams to push the boundaries of what's

possible. By charting a bold course, they set the stage for innovation and transformation.

3. **Empower Your Leadership Team.** Change management is a team sport, and assembling a diverse, cohesive group of change agents is critical to success. These creative individuals will help drive the change agenda—fostering trust, collaboration, and a shared sense of ownership.

4. **Explore External Context.** To navigate the ever-shifting landscape of the modern business world, change champions must be attuned to the external realities that shape their industries. This means assessing market trends, competition, and customer needs, as well as identifying opportunities and threats in the broader ecosystem.

5. **Examine Internal Capabilities.** Change influencers must also look inward, assessing their organizations' strengths and weaknesses while leveraging existing resources to drive strategic advantage. This involves cultivating a culture of innovation and continuous improvement, turning challenges into opportunities for growth.

6. **Establish Resource Allocation.** Leaders must ensure that resources—financial, human, and technological—are allocated according to strategic priorities. This requires balancing short-term and long-term investments, as well as maintaining agility and flexibility in resource allocation.

7. **Execute Strategic Action.** With a clear vision and the necessary resources in place, leaders must develop and implement a comprehensive, actionable change roadmap. This involves executing change initiatives with focus and discipline, monitoring progress, and adjusting course as needed.

8. **Encourage the Heart.** Change can be daunting, but great leaders know how to ignite passion and commitment in

their teams. By creating a sense of urgency, recognizing and rewarding change champions, and celebrating milestones, they cultivate an atmosphere of excitement and enthusiasm.

9. **Evaluate the Results.** To ensure and measure the success of their change efforts, leaders must establish clear metrics and indicators, conduct regular performance reviews, and learn from both successes and failures. This process of continuous evaluation enables them to refine their strategies and drive ongoing improvement.

10. **Evolutionary Process.** Change-focused leadership is an ongoing journey—not a single adjustment. By fostering a culture of continuous learning and adaptation, embedding change and innovation into the organizational DNA, and preparing for future disruptions, leaders can sustain momentum and keep their organizations ahead of the curve.

With these ten elements as their guide, leaders can embrace and handle the challenge of change. They can harness its transformative power to reshape their organizations and chart a bold course toward a brighter and more innovative tomorrow.

Reflective Questions: The Necessity of Change

1. How has the business landscape evolved in recent years, and why is adaptability crucial for success?

2. What are some examples of companies that failed to adapt to change, and what lessons can be learned from their experience?

3. How do you define change leadership, and why is it critical in today's business world?

4. What role does resilience play in organizational change?

5. Can you recall a time when you experienced significant change in your personal or professional life? How did you handle it?

6. How does your organization currently respond to shifts in the external context, and what can be improved in this regard?

7. Reflecting on the ten elements, which ones do you believe your organization excels at, and which ones require more attention for successful change leadership?

1.
Embrace Change:
Cultivating a Growth Mindset

In the dynamic dance of business, the steps of learning, unlearning, and relearning are the rhythm that keeps us moving forward.

— Christopher Meade, PhD

Adaptability and Resilience

Picture this: You're a tightrope walker, balancing precariously on a thin wire suspended high above the ground. Oh, yes, and there are high winds. Daunting. How do you stay balanced? Simple—with adaptability and resilience.

In the face of the winds of constant change, the ability to bend without breaking (or falling) is more important than ever. Like a willow tree that sways steadily in the storm but never snaps, great change leaders possess the adaptability and resilience needed to weather the ups and downs of the modern business world in its constant state of flux.

Adaptability is about staying agile, nimble, and responsive. It's about adjusting your sails to catch the shifting winds of change, having the foresight and flexibility to pivot on a dime, and embracing new ideas and approaches that act as propellers for your organization. In essence, adaptability is a vital key to survival in today's business climate.

Resilience is the ability to bounce back in the face of adversity, to pick yourself up, dust yourself off, and forge ahead with renewed determination. It comes down to cultivating a mindset of grit and perseverance. We must possess an unwavering belief in the power of persistence. Like the mythical phoenix that rises from the ashes, resilient transformational leaders emerge stronger, wiser, and more determined in the face of setbacks and challenges. In fact, we *expect* setbacks and challenges —and then we *embrace* them.

Creating a Change Culture

If adaptability and resilience are the secret sauce of change leadership, how can leaders infuse these qualities into the very fabric of their organizations? The answer lies in creating a culture that indeed *does* embrace change—a vibrant ecosystem where innovation thrives. That's where new ideas take root.

Below are some tips for cultivating a change-friendly culture:

1. **Foster a growth mindset.** This is an attitude that views challenges as opportunities for growth and improvement, encouraging employees to take risks, learn from their mistakes, and see failures as stepping stones on the road to success.

2. **Encourage open communication.** Leaders must foster communication channels that promote the free flow of ideas and information. This encourages employees to speak up, share their opinions, and contribute their insights without fear of judgment or reprisal.

3. **Empower employees.** When employees feel empowered to take ownership of their work, they're more likely to embrace change and contribute to an organization's transformation. Encourage employees to take the initiative and make decisions, and you'll inspire them to drive innovation at every level of the organization.

4. **Celebrate innovation.** If you want your organization to embrace change, you need to celebrate and reward innovation. Recognize and applaud employees who come up with new ideas, challenge the status quo, and push boundaries.

5. **Provide training and support.** Change can be disorienting and overwhelming, but providing employees with the necessary training and support can help ease transitions. Offer resources, tools, and learning opportunities to help them adapt to new technologies, processes, and ways of working.

Apple's Odyssey: From Garage to Dominance

Apple is a terrific example of a company that didn't *just* create innovative products. Rather, it understood and stayed (way) ahead of consumer needs and desires—and made embracing change almost second nature. The company has always placed significant emphasis on the user experience, ensuring that its products are not only groundbreaking but also intuitive and user-friendly. The seamless integration between hardware, software, and services has given Apple an arguably unparalleled edge. Every product or service is designed to work perfectly within the Apple ecosystem, which provides its consumers with a unified and consistent experience.

One of Apple's strengths is its ability to enter established markets and redefine them. Before the iPod, there were numerous MP3 players in the market. But it was Apple's unique combination of hardware (iPod), software (iTunes), and content (music) that revolutionized the music industry. Similarly, the smartphone market certainly existed before the iPhone, but Apple's introduction of a device that combined an iPod, a phone, and an "Internet communication device" altered the game entirely. It didn't just embrace change—it *was* the change.

The company's retail strategy has also been a significant part of its success. Apple Stores, with their minimalist design and Genius Bars, provide customers with an opportunity to tangibly experience the brand. These spaces serve not just as retail outlets but also as community hubs where users can learn, explore, mingle, and get support.

Furthermore, Apple's commitment to privacy and sustainability demonstrates its forward-thinking approach. In a digital age fraught with concerns about data misuse, Apple has been a champion of user privacy. Similarly, its push toward a closed-loop supply chain and the use of recycled materials in its products highlight its commitment to sustainable practices.

Apple's ethos, summed up in its famous "Think Different" campaign, speaks to its contrarian approach, its willingness to break norms, and its relentless drive to set new standards—essentially, to *change*. From its early days in a Los Altos garage to its global presence today, Apple's journey exemplifies the power of a growth mindset and the importance of embracing the flux in the rapidly evolving world of technology. By embracing change and relentlessly pursuing innovation, Apple has become one of the world's most valuable and recognizable brands.

Recognizing and Overcoming Resistance

Resistance to change is a human instinct—a primal reaction rooted in our innate fear of the unknown. But while resistance may be an inevitable part of the change process, it's not insurmountable. By recognizing the signs of resistance and addressing them directly, change leaders can help their organizations overcome the barriers to change. They can chart a course toward a brighter, more innovative future.

Let's explore some strategies for recognizing and overcoming resistance to change.

1. **Listen and empathize.** One of the most effective ways to combat resistance to change is to listen and empathize with those who are struggling to adapt. By acknowledging their concerns and validating their feelings, we can help ease their fears and build trust in the change process. For instance, after rolling out a new software system, a manager notices that one of her team members seems particularly frustrated. Rather than dismissing his concerns or pushing him to adapt quickly, she schedules a one-on-one meeting. During the discussion, the team member expresses his anxiety about learning the new platform and worries about its impact on his daily tasks. The manager validates his concerns, assures him that his feelings are valid, and promises continued support throughout the transition.

2. **Communicate the "why."** People are more likely to embrace change when they understand the reasons behind it and its potential benefits. As a thought leader, clearly communicate the rationale for the change, and explain the goals you're trying to achieve and how they'll benefit the organization *and* its employees. For example, a company decides to switch to a remote working model to tap into a broader talent pool and trim overhead. The leadership doesn't merely announce the change—they hold town-hall meetings where they clearly explain their reasons behind this shift, the long-term vision for the company, and how it benefits both the organization and the employees' work-life balance.

3. **Involve employees in the change process.** Resistance to change often stems from a feeling of powerlessness, exclusion, or lack of control. By involving employees in the change process, you give them a sense of ownership and agency, and this makes them more likely to support and champion the change. For instance, before redesigning the office workspace, a company creates a committee with rep-

resentatives from every department. The committee provides feedback on the proposed designs, and makes suggestions on what they believe would enhance productivity and employee satisfaction. This inclusivity makes the final design more accepted among everyone.

4. **Address the "WIIFM?" ("What's in it for me?") factor.** When change is in the air, every person naturally wonders what's in it for them. Answer this question by highlighting the personal benefits of the change, such as opportunities for growth, skill development, or career advancement. Let's say that a firm is shifting to a new client management system. To encourage uptake, the company emphasizes how this system will reduce the time employees spend on data entry, streamline client communications, and even offer insights that could help in personal career growth within client-management roles.

5. **Provide support and resources.** Change can be intimidating, but providing employees with the support and resources they need to adapt helps ease the transition. Offer training, mentorship, and other resources to help them build the skills and confidence they need to navigate the changing landscape. For example, let's say that a school is introducing a new digital teaching platform. Understanding that some teachers might be less tech-savvy than others, the administration offers workshops and written guides. They even appoint a mentor for each department to ensure that everyone is comfortable and confident with the new system.

6. **Be patient and persistent.** Overcoming resistance to change takes time and persistence. Stay the course, even when the going gets tough, reminding employees that change is a journey—not a destination. Celebrate small victories and milestones to help maintain momentum and

enthusiasm for that change. Let's imagine that a healthcare facility is introducing a new patient record system. After the initial rollout, they encounter significant pushback and a host of problems. Instead of reverting to the old system, the leadership reaffirms the reasons for the change, acknowledging the problems and seeking regular feedback. They make incremental changes based on this feedback, and then they hold monthly check-ins and celebrate when departments make significant strides in adopting the new system.

Embracing change and cultivating a growth mindset are essential for success in today's dynamic business landscape. By developing adaptability and resilience, fostering a culture that embraces change, and recognizing and overcoming resistance, leaders can chart a course toward a more innovative and transformative future. So go ahead: Take the plunge and dive headfirst into the exhilarating waters of change.

Reflective Questions: Embracing Change

1. How do you define a growth mindset? Why is it essential for embracing change?

2. What are some ways to cultivate a growth mindset within your organization?

3. How can leaders create a culture that embraces change?

4. What are the potential consequences of failing to embrace change in a business setting?

5. Can you think of any examples of when embracing change led to significant innovation and success for your company?

6. How do personal biases or preconceived notions play a role in resisting change? How can leaders address and overcome these biases to ensure successful transformation?

7. In times when change initiatives don't yield the expected outcomes, how should leaders reassess and pivot their strategies to maintain trust and momentum within the organization?

2.
Envision the Future:
Charting a Bold Course

In the vast sea of business, it's not enough to ride
the waves—we must chart the stars, set our sails, and
journey toward horizons of our own making.

— Christopher Meade, PhD

Crafting a Compelling Vision

Imagine you're the captain of a mighty ship, sailing the uncharted waters of the modern business world. To guide your vessel and crew through the tempestuous seas, you need a destination—a shining beacon on the horizon that provides scope and focus for all aboard. This is your vision for change. It's a powerful and captivating image of the future that inspires and motivates your team to embark on the adventure of a lifetime. Change doesn't have to be scary. In fact, it should be a welcomed adventure.

So then, how do you craft a vision that ignites the spark of transformation? How do you create a rallying cry that resonates with your crew and excitingly propels your ship forward?

Let's look at some recommendations for crafting a compelling vision for change.

1. **Make it aspirational.** A great vision should inspire and energize your team. It should paint a vivid picture of a future that's worth fighting for. Think big and boldly. Stretch the boundaries of what's possible, and dare to dream of a better tomorrow.

2. **Keep it simple and clear.** While your vision should be ambitious, it should also be simple and clear—a concise and memorable statement that cuts through noise and captures the essence of your carefully sketched future.

3. **Root it in your organization's core values and purpose.** To truly resonate with your team, your vision should be grounded in the values and purpose that define your organization. Connect the dots between your change efforts and your broader mission and goals. Demonstrate how your vision aligns with and advances your core principles.

4. **Make it tangible and specific.** A vague vision is unlikely to inspire much enthusiasm or commitment, so strive to be concrete and specific, with clear goals and milestones that your team can rally around.

5. **Communicate it consistently and passionately.** A vision is only as powerful as the leader who communicates it. Share your vision with passion, conviction, and enthusiasm while weaving it into the fabric of your organization's culture and communications.

Audacious Goals and Aspirations

With a compelling vision in place, you can now chart a course toward your destination by setting audacious goals and aspirations that stretch your organization's capabilities and push the boundaries of what's possible. Like the North Star that guides sailors on their epic voyages, these goals are your crew's beacon, illuminating the way forward for your change efforts.

Below are some ideas for setting audacious goals and aspirations.

1. **Think big and boldly.** When setting goals, don't be afraid to swing for the fence. Aim high and embrace the chal-

lenge; set ambitious targets that stretch your organization's abilities and drive innovation.

2. **Build manageable milestones.** While your goals should be audacious, they should also be achievable—and divisible. Break them down into smaller, more manageable milestones. Provide a clear roadmap for progress and a sense of momentum while the team ventures toward the ultimate destination.

3. **Align your goals with your vision and values.** Ensure that your goals and aspirations are in sync with your broader vision and values. Reinforce the connection between your change efforts and the overall mission and purpose of your organization.

4. **Mix short-term and long-term goals.** Striking a balance between short-term and long-term goals is crucial for maintaining momentum and motivation. Yes, it's important to set your sights on the horizon, but don't forget to celebrate the small victories and milestones along the way.

5. **Create a sense of urgency and commitment.** To drive action and progress, instill a sense of urgency and commitment around your goals. Set deadlines, hold your team accountable, and provide the support and resources they need to succeed.

Tesla's Electrifying Revolution

There is, arguably, no greater modern example of a change-embracing company than Tesla. It's built its success on a bold and audacious mission to accelerate the world's transition to sustainable energy. At the heart of its meteoric rise lies a commitment to innovation and a refusal to be constrained by the status quo. It appears to be a veritable quicksilver company—not merely focused on creating electric cars but also on redefining what a car can be. Its vehicles are often described as computers on wheels, emphasizing its revolutionary approach to car design—merging hardware, software, and cutting-edge technology.

Tesla's Model S, for instance, challenged the prevailing narrative that electric vehicles couldn't match or exceed the performance or luxury of their gasoline counterparts. It swiftly set new standards for electric vehicle (EV) acceleration, range, and safety, forever altering perceptions of what electric cars could achieve.

Beyond vehicles, Tesla has reshaped the energy-solutions landscape by demonstrating its holistic approach to a sustainable future. Its acquisition of SolarCity and the development of the Powerwall and Solar Roof products underscore its vision to offer end-to-end green energy solutions, from generation to consumption. Tesla, remarkably, is capable of having *multiple* beacons for its astounding teams.

And the changes don't end there. Tesla engages in direct-to-consumer sales, bypassing traditional dealership models and benefitting buyers. This ingenious tactic not only disrupts the auto industry's conventional sales paradigm—it also allows for a closer relationship with consumers. This model has fostered a strong and loyal customer base, with Tesla owners often being the company's most vocal evangelists—so much so that Tesla rarely needs to engage in advertising like its competitors.

Tesla's Gigafactories are another testament to its vision and scale. Designed to achieve both massive output and a net-zero energy footprint, these factories significantly ramp up production of batteries and cars while minimizing its environmental impact.

Culture and work ethic are also pivotal to Tesla's narrative. The company's intense pace and demand for excellence—sometimes dubbed the "Tesla Stretch"—represent an environment where boundaries are continuously pushed. This approach has its detractors, but many see it as a necessary ethos for a company set on ushering in a future that was previously unimaginable.

Tesla isn't merely an automaker or an energy company; it's the vanguard of a movement toward a more sustainable, interconnected, and technologically advanced future. The company's holistic approach, audacity, and commitment to innovation have made it more than just a brand—it's a beacon for what's possible in the realm of sustainable technology and transport.

With its extraordinarily clear vision, Tesla has overcome numerous obstacles and setbacks. By envisioning a bold future, the company has positioned itself as a leader in the global push toward clean energy and sustainable transportation.

Creating a Shared Future

With a bold vision and audacious goals in place, you can now rally the troops and align your organization around a shared future. That means bringing everyone on board. A compelling vision creates a sense of unity and shared purpose, transcending functional silos and uniting your team in pursuit of a common goal.

Let's examine some best practices for aligning your organization around a shared future.

1. **Communicate vision and goals effectively.** Use multiple channels and formats to share your message and tailor communications to different audiences within your organization. This creates a sense of alignment and shared purpose. Apple has always been adept at these strategies—with both its employees and the public. In the early days, Steve Jobs' vision was to create an "insanely great" computer. He effectively communicated this by introducing the Macintosh with a dramatic public event and internal pep talks, ensuring that everyone from engineers to marketers under-

stood the company's direction—its *raison d'être*. As Apple grew, its vision expanded, and the mission morphed to create products at the intersection of art and technology. Its product launches, led by detailed and charismatic presentations, are a testament to its ability to communicate a vision effectively.

2. **Involve employees in the process.** Foster a sense of ownership and commitment by including employees in the crafting and refining of vision and goals. Solicit their input and feedback, and encourage them to take an active role in shaping the future of your organization. Atlassian, an Australian enterprise software company, does this quite well. It runs "ShipIt Days," formerly known as "FedEx Days," where employees get 24 hours to work on any project they choose, as long as it's not part of their regular jobs. When finished, they present (or "ship") their projects. Many of these innovations have become part of Atlassian's products or internal tools. This initiative not only ignites creativity and innovation but also fosters a strong sense of ownership as employees are able to see their ideas come to life. "ShipIt Days" has given birth to many features and tools that are now integral parts of the Atlassian ecosystem.

3. **Build cross-functional teams.** Foster collaboration by creating different teams that work together toward shared goals, encouraging the sharing of learning and insights with the broader organization. Create a culture of knowledge-sharing and continuous improvement. Spotify uses a model of "squads," "tribes," "chapters," and "guilds" to foster collaboration. Each squad is like a mini startup with its own autonomous mission, often with members from various functions, creating a blend of skills and perspectives. The broader structures like tribes and guilds allow these squads to coordinate and share insights.

4. **Align incentives and rewards.** Recognize and celebrate employees who clearly contribute to the achievement of your vision and goals, and provide opportunities for growth and advancement to those who demonstrate a commitment to the change effort. Zappos, the online shoe and clothing retailer, does this like few others. It offers undesirable new-hires money to quit after their initial training is over to ensure that only those truly committed to the company's unique service-focused culture remain. This aligns with Zappos' emphasis on customer service and ensures that employees are genuinely invested in the vision.

5. **Monitor progress and adjust course as needed.** Establish clear success metrics and indicators, conducting regular performance reviews to ensure that your organization remains on track and aligned with your desired future. 3M follows a model where it aims to derive 30% of its revenues from products introduced in the previous four years. This ensures that the company is continuously innovating and staying relevant. Regular reviews are held to check progress against this metric. If certain units or products aren't aligning with this vision, strategic shifts are made to keep the organization on its toes and ensure alignment with the vision of continual innovation.

Envisioning the future is a critical component of successful forward-thinking leadership. Crafting a compelling vision is part of the process, as well as setting audacious goals and aspirations. Aligning your organization around a shared future is key—it inspires and motivates your team, who can then embrace the challenge of change and embark on a transformative journey toward a brighter, more innovative tomorrow. It's time to hoist the sails, man the helm, and let the winds of change propel your ship onwards. Your bold new future awaits.

Reflective Questions: Envisioning the Future

1. What are the key elements of crafting a compelling vision for change?

2. Why is it important for leaders to set audacious goals and aspirations?

3. How can leaders align their organizations around a shared future?

4. What challenges might leaders face when trying to create and communicate a bold vision for the future?

5. How can leaders inspire others to buy into their vision for change?

6. Considering the fast-changing dynamics of today's world, how often should an organization revisit its vision and goals to ensure relevance?

7. How do the core values of your organization influence and shape its vision for the future? How can you ensure that these values are consistently reflected in the journey toward this vision?

3.
Empower the Leadership Team: Assembling a Cohesive Force

In the realm of leadership, every team member possesses a unique superpower. When united, they become the Avengers of innovation and change.
— Christopher Meade, PhD

Building a Team of Change Agents

Imagine you're assembling an elite team of superheroes, each with their unique powers and abilities, united in a quest to save the world. In the realm of change leadership, your empowered leadership team is just like this superhero squad: a dynamic force of diverse and complementary talents united in their mission toward transformation and innovation.

But how do you build such a formidable team? The following are some considerations for assembling a diverse and complementary team of change agents:

1. **Seek diversity in skills, experiences, and perspectives.** When building your leadership team, acquire a rich tapestry of skills and experiences. Value perspectives that reflect the complexity and diversity of your organization. By embracing diversity, you can harness the power of collective intelligence and spark creative problem solving.

2. **Look for complementary strengths.** Like a complex machine, an empowered leadership team should have complementary strengths that bridge gaps and create a synergistic

effect. Seek out team members who excel in areas where others may be weak, and create a balanced and well-rounded team that's equipped to tackle any challenge.

3. **Value emotional intelligence.** While technical expertise is crucial, don't underestimate the importance of emotional intelligence in transformational change. Look for team members who possess empathy, self-awareness, and strong interpersonal skills. These are essential for building trust, fostering collaboration, and navigating the emotional complexities of change.

4. **Prioritize adaptability and resilience.** As the saying goes, "Change is the only constant." To lead your organization through the whirlwind of transformation, your team must be adaptable. It must be able to pivot, persevere, and bounce back in the face of setbacks and challenges.

5. **Emphasize a growth mindset.** Finally, seek out team members who embrace an attitude that views challenges as opportunities for improvement. These individuals will more likely approach change with curiosity and enthusiasm, driving innovation and continuous learning.

Fostering Trust and Collaboration

With your superhero squad assembled, you can now cultivate a strong sense of trust and collaboration among its members. Like the invisible glue that binds your team together, trust is the foundation upon which effective teamwork and collaboration are built.

Below are some action items for fostering trust and collaboration among your leadership team.

1. **Lead by example.** As the leader, you must set the tone for trust and collaboration. Be open, transparent, and authen-

tic in your communications. Demonstrate your commitment to teamwork by actively listening, sharing your own ideas and opinions, and valuing others' contributions.

2. **Encourage open communication.** Create an environment where team members feel comfortable sharing thoughts, ideas, and concerns without fear of judgment or reprisal. Encourage open and honest dialogue by emphasizing the importance of constructive feedback and active listening.

3. **Promote shared goals and values.** Align your team around a set of shared goals and values that reflects your organization's vision and purpose, as this creates a sense of unity and common purpose. Encourage a collaborative mindset and a sense of collective responsibility for the change effort.

4. **Foster psychological safety.** Psychological safety makes us feel like we can take risks, speak up, and make mistakes without fear of negative consequences. Create a safe space for your team to experiment, learn, and grow. Celebrate failures as opportunities for growth and learning.

5. **Cultivate a team identity.** Develop a shared sense of identity and pride among your team members by establishing team rituals, traditions, and symbols that reinforce your team's unique culture and values.

Google's Visionary Voyage

It's a fair assumption that everyone in the developed world knows Google, with a leadership model embedded in its renowned "10x thinking." Instead of seeking a somewhat-standard 10% improvement on an existing process or product, Google strives for a tenfold improvement. It's audacious thinking—and it isn't just promoted but expected from its leadership team. It's generated products like

Google Glass, the self-driving car initiative under Waymo, and advancements in artificial intelligence with DeepMind.

Google's leadership also has the principle of "freedom within a framework," which led to the birth of its famous "20% time." This initiative allowed Googlers (employees) to spend 20% of their time working on what they believe will most benefit the company. It not only empowered them with a sense of ownership but also led to the creation of many of Google's innovative products like Google News, AdSense, and even Gmail.

Google's leadership understands the importance of fostering a learning culture. Its internal educational program "Google U" offers courses on everything from coding and machine-learning to public speaking, emphasizing the leadership's commitment to continuous growth and development. This has helped Google attract and retain some of the best talent globally. They not only offer the opportunity to work on groundbreaking projects but they also contend for an environment that champions learning and personal development.

Transparency is another pillar of Google's leadership model. Regular "TGIF" meetings were held, where founders Larry Page, Sergey Brin, and other top executives would update Googlers on company news and answer questions in an open format. A practice such as this instills a sense of trust and bridges any potential gaps between leadership and employees.

Google's leadership also prioritizes the well-being and happiness of employees. Recognizing that happy employees are more productive, Google has incorporated features like massage rooms, bowling alleys, and organic restaurants in its offices. It's set a benchmark for providing a holistic work environment that blends work and play.

The leadership doesn't just set the direction—it sets the tone for the entire company. Through its inclusive, innovative, and forward-thinking approach, Google has built an empire that's as much about pushing technological boundaries as it is about nurturing the next generation of leaders and thinkers.

Collective Accountability and Ownership

With trust and collaboration in full swing, it's time to empower your team by cultivating a collective sense of accountability and ownership. This fosters a culture where every team member feels responsible for the success of the change effort and is committed to doing their part to bring your vision to life.

Let's look at some strategies for cultivating a collective sense of accountability and ownership among your leadership team.

1. **Set clear expectations and goals.** Ensure that everyone understands their roles and responsibilities in the change effort. This helps create a sense of shared responsibility and focus, driving your team toward collective success. For example, before launching a new project, you could host a kick-off meeting where you use a visual roadmap to outline the project's goals, key milestones, and individual responsibilities. You'd then provide a printed copy of this roadmap to each team member, ensuring that everyone has a clear understanding of what's expected of them and the project's objectives.

2. **Involve team members in decision making.** A sense of ownership and commitment to the change process involves your team shaping the direction of the change effort, thus creating a sense of buy-in and shared purpose. Consider this approach: Instead of deciding on a new software tool for the team on your own, you could set up a demo session with the software vendor and invite all team members. After the demo, you'd organize a feedback session where everyone can voice their opinions and concerns. Based on

collective feedback, the decision is made on whether or not to proceed with the purchase.

3. **Hold each other accountable.** Your team members could conduct regular check-ins, performance reviews, and peer feedback about one another's actions and commitments, creating a culture of accountability and continuous improvement. For instance, you could introduce a monthly review session where each team member shares updates on their tasks and projects. If there are delays or issues, the team collaboratively finds solutions. This practice not only keeps everyone on track but also encourages open communication about challenges, and it also offers peer-to-peer support.

4. **Celebrate successes and learn from failures.** Recognize and celebrate your team's achievements, both big and small, and use setbacks and failures as opportunities for growth and learning. By reinforcing a sense of collective accomplishment and progress, you'll foster a culture of ownership and pride. For example, at the end of a successful project, you could organize a small celebration like a lunch or an evening out. But when a project doesn't go as planned, you could organize a "lessons learned" meeting. Instead of pointing fingers, the team discusses what went wrong, how they can avoid similar mistakes, and what they can learn from the experience.

5. **Foster autonomy and empowerment.** Give your team members the independence and authority they need to make decisions, solve problems, and drive innovation. By empowering your team to take ownership of their work, you unleash their full potential and create a powerful force for change. Seeing a need for a more streamlined communication process, a team member might suggest the adoption of a new messaging platform. Instead of making the

decision yourself, you could encourage the team member to research the best options, test them out, and present a proposal to the team. The team member would feel trusted and empowered to take charge of this initiative, and the entire team will benefit from the improved communication tool.

Assembling an empowered leadership team is a vital ingredient in the recipe for successful, growth-centered leadership. By building a diverse and complementary team of change agents, fostering trust and collaboration among team members, and cultivating a collective sense of accountability and ownership, you'll create a cohesive force that's ready to tackle the challenges of transformation and innovation head-on.

Reflective Questions: Assembling a Cohesive Team

1. Why is it important to build a diverse and complementary team of change agents?

2. What are some strategies for fostering trust and collaboration among team members?

3. How can leaders cultivate a collective sense of accountability and ownership within their teams?

4. What challenges might a leadership team face when navigating change?

5. How can leaders ensure that their team remains focused and aligned throughout the change process?

6. How do personal values and individual leadership styles impact the dynamics and effectiveness of a leadership team?

7. In what ways can continuous learning and development opportunities further enhance the cohesion and effectiveness of your leadership team?

4.
Explore External Context:
Deciphering the Business Landscape

Just as a detective decodes hidden messages, in business we must decipher the subtle cues of our market and align ourselves with allies to crack the case of success.

— Christopher Meade, PhD

Market Trends, Competition, and Customer Needs

Attention, change influencers: Picture yourself as a master detective, scouring the constantly changing business landscape for clues, deciphering hidden patterns, and piecing together the puzzle of your market and industry. To navigate the swirling waters of change and disruption, it's crucial to have a deep understanding of the external context in which your organization operates—including market trends, competition, and customer needs.

Below are some tips for assessing the external context of your business:

1. **Be a trend spotter.** Keep a finger on the pulse of your industry by staying up to date on the latest trends, technologies, and innovations. Subscribe to industry newsletters, attend conferences and events, and network with other professionals to stay informed. Gain valuable insights by keeping your mind's eye always open to new information.

2. **Know your competition.** Keep an eye on your competitors, monitoring their strategies, strengths, and weaknesses

to identify potential opportunities and threats. Conduct a thorough competitive analysis to better understand your position in the market, and uncover areas where you can differentiate and create a competitive advantage.

3. **Get up close and personal with your customers.** Dive deep into the world of your customers to understand their needs, preferences, and pain points. Use surveys, interviews, and focus groups to gather feedback and insights, and always stay abreast of changing customer expectations and demands.

4. **Look beyond your industry.** Don't limit your analysis to your immediate industry or sector. Seek inspiration and insights from other industries and markets, as disruptive forces and trends often emerge from unexpected sources.

5. **Embrace data and analytics.** Harness the power of data and analytics to uncover hidden patterns, trends, and opportunities in the market. Use market research, predictive analytics, and customer segmentation to inform your decision making and sharpen your competitive edge.

Identifying Opportunities and Threats

With a thorough understanding of your external context, it's time to channel your inner Sherlock Holmes so that you can hone your assessments of opportunities and threats in the business ecosystem. Like a master chess player, you must anticipate the moves of your competitors, customers, and stakeholders. It's critical to learn how to identify potential openings and challenges that could shape the future of your organization.

Let's look at some suggestions for identifying opportunities and threats in your business ecosystem.

1. **Conduct a SWOT analysis.** A SWOT (strengths, weaknesses, opportunities, and threats) analysis helps you evaluate your organization's internal and external context. By examining the intersection of your team's SWOT factors, you can identify strategic priorities, as well as areas for growth and improvement.

2. **Keep an eye on emerging technologies.** Stay abreast of emerging technologies and innovations that could disrupt—or grow—your industry. Explore potential applications for these technologies within your organization, and consider how they might impact your business model, operations, and competitive landscape.

3. **Monitor regulatory and political changes.** Keep a close watch on the regulatory and political environment, as changes in laws, regulations, and policies can significantly impact your organization. Proactively anticipate and adapt to these changes, considering how they might create opportunities or challenges for your business.

4. **Assess the impact of social and environmental factors.** Consider the broader factors that could influence your organization's success, such as shifting demographics, consumer values, and sustainability concerns. Evaluate how these trends might present opportunities or threats, and incorporate these insights into your strategic planning and decision making.

5. **Foster a culture of curiosity and continuous learning.** Empower your team to explore new ideas, trends, and opportunities. By fostering this type of open/growth culture and mindset, you'll create a more agile and adaptive organization that's better equipped to navigate the complexities of the external context.

Amazon's Odyssey

Amazon stands out as a trailblazer that's effectively deciphered the business landscape. Its strategy goes beyond mere market observation—the company is notorious for its customer obsession and willingness to be misunderstood, as Jeff Bezos has often said. This dedication to understanding and anticipating customer needs has allowed it to innovate and offer services even before the market realized a demand for them. The creation of Amazon Prime is an excellent example. Originally introduced as a two-day shipping service, it was an expensive gamble that customers would pay upfront for faster delivery. As it turns out, the company did, indeed, accurately decipher its customers' desires. Today, Prime boasts over 200 million members worldwide and offers an expanded suite of benefits, from streaming to special discounts.

Amazon also has built an internal culture of embracing failures. Bezos believed that to innovate, one must be willing to fail. This philosophy led to the creation of platforms like AWS (Amazon Web Services). Originally designed to manage Amazon's information infrastructure, AWS evolved into a full-fledged outside service, making Amazon the largest cloud-service provider globally.

The company's foray into devices also showcases its strategic vision. The Kindle wasn't just an e-reader but a (successful) strategy to digitize the book industry. Its Amazon Echo and voice assistant Alexa marked Amazon's entry into the smart-home ecosystem, which helped to further embed the company into consumers' daily lives.

Amazon's retail strategy has been commendable as well. Recognizing the continued value of physical retail, Amazon ventured into brick-and-mortar stores with Amazon Go that introduced a checkout-free shopping experience. And the acquisition of Whole Foods further expanded its physical footprint, which gave Amazon a strong position in the grocery sector.

Amazon's prowess lies not just in adapting to the external environment but also in shaping it. Its forward-thinking initiatives, combined with a robust understanding of consumer behavior and a willingness to take risks, have positioned it as a vanguard in the global retail arena.

By continually scanning and deciphering the business landscape for opportunities and threats, Amazon has transformed itself into a global powerhouse that spans e-commerce, cloud computing, digital media, and more. The company's ability to explore and adapt to the external context has been a key factor in its ongoing success and dominance.

Leveraging External Partnerships and Alliances

No superhero is complete without trusty sidekicks, and the same goes for change architects. In today's interconnected world, it's often necessary to join forces with external partners and allies to achieve your goals and navigate the challenges of the business landscape.

Below are some recommendations for leveraging external partnerships and alliances to drive change and innovation.

1. **Identify strategic partners.** Seek out partners who share your vision and values. Do they complement your organization's strengths and capabilities? Look for partners that bring unique expertise, resources, or market access that can help you achieve your strategic objectives. Create ways to ensure a win-win scenario for both parties. Imagine that you run a sustainable-clothing brand, and to truly amplify your sustainability efforts, you seek a partnership with an eco-friendly dye manufacturer. This not only aligns with your brand's ethos but also gives your clothing a unique selling proposition in the market. Their expertise in eco-

dyes complements your sustainable fabric, creating a win-win situation where both of you benefit.

2. **Establish clear goals and expectations.** Before entering a partnership or alliance, establish clear objectives for both parties. This will align your collaboration with your strategic goals and reduce the risk of misunderstandings or misaligned priorities. Let's suppose that you run a tech start-up focusing on fitness apps. Before collaborating with a smartwatch manufacturer, you both decide that the main goal is to integrate your app seamlessly with their latest smartwatch. You set clear timelines, deliverables, and mutual benefits, ensuring no room for ambiguity.

3. **Foster open communication and trust.** Like any relationship, successful partnerships and alliances require regular and clear channels of communication. Be transparent and honest in your interactions, helping to build a strong foundation of trust and mutual respect that'll enable your collaboration to flourish. For example, let's say that you're managing a travel agency aiming to offer unique local experiences, and you partner with local artisans and tour guides. From the get-go, you establish monthly meetings, provide platforms for instant communication, and share honest feedback, making sure that both sides feel heard, understood, and valued.

4. **Be flexible and adaptive.** Partnerships and alliances can be complex and dynamic, requiring a high degree of flexibility and adaptability from all parties. Be prepared to adjust your approach and expectations, and be open to learning and evolving together with your partner. For instance, imagine that you're a restaurateur looking to introduce a new global cuisine and you collaborate with an experienced regional chef. As both of you blend your expertise, there might be differences in opinion on menu items or presentation. In-

stead of rigidly sticking to your initial vision, you're able to adapt to and fuse both perspectives, resulting in a more authentic and innovative dining experience.

5. **Evaluate and measure success.** Regularly evaluate the success of your partnership or alliance, using both qualitative and quantitative metrics to assess your progress toward shared goals. This will help to ensure that your collaboration remains on track and delivers the desired results for both parties. Let's say that you own a bookstore and form an alliance with a local coffee shop to start a book cafe. Every quarter, both of you sit down to review the footfall, sales, and customer feedback. Using these metrics, you're able to gauge the success of your collaboration, identifying areas of improvement and celebrating shared victories.

Exploring the external context is a critical component of successful transformation-oriented leadership. By assessing market trends, competition, and customer needs; identifying opportunities and threats in the ecosystem; and leveraging external partnerships and alliances, you'll be well equipped to decipher the business landscape and chart a course toward a brighter, more innovative future.

Reflective Questions: Deciphering the Business Landscape

1. Why is it important for leaders to assess market trends, competition, and customer needs?

2. How can leaders identify opportunities and threats in their business ecosystem?

3. What role do external partnerships and alliances play in strategic change?

4. How can leaders stay ahead of the curve when it comes to understanding their external context?

5. Can you think of an example of a time when your company successfully leveraged external factors to drive change?

6. How can fostering a culture of curiosity within an organization influence its adaptability to external changes?

7. In what ways might blind spots in understanding the external business landscape adversely affect an organization's growth and innovation strategy?

5.
Examine Internal Capabilities: Unearthing Hidden Potential

Our internal strengths are like hidden treasures. By mapping them out and digging deep, we uncover the gold that propels us ahead in business.

— Christopher Meade, PhD

Organizational Strengths and Weaknesses

Change initiators, it's time to embark on an exhilarating treasure hunt within your organization. The hour is here to unearth the hidden gems and secret strengths that lie beneath the surface. Just as the external context is vital to understanding your place in the business landscape, evaluating your organization's internal capabilities is crucial to charting a course for growth, innovation, and transformation.

Below, let's examine how to assess your organization's strengths and weaknesses.

1. **Conduct a thorough organizational audit.** Like a skilled archaeologist, dig deep into your organization's structure, processes, and culture to uncover areas of strength and weakness. Examine leadership, talent, technology, and financial resources to obtain a comprehensive picture of your organization's capabilities—its full potential. To illustrate, let's say that you're heading the operations department in a retail company, and you've observed fluctuating sales in the past quarters. To pinpoint the cause, you decide to audit the entire supply chain. By plotting each stage, from supplier

contracts to in-store arrangements, you begin to identify bottlenecks that affect product availability. You also discover certain strengths, such as a dedicated purchasing team, and weaknesses, like outdated inventory management software. Armed with this knowledge, you can now focus on overhauling the software to further streamline operations.

2. **Seek feedback from employees.** Dig into the treasure trove of collective wisdom within your workforce by soliciting feedback on your organization's strengths, weaknesses, and opportunities for improvement. Use surveys, focus groups, and one-on-one interviews to gather valuable insights from employees at all levels of the organization. For example, let's say that you're the leader of a design team and have noticed varied quality in output, but you're a bit baffled as to why. To gather the firsthand experiences of your team members, you launch an anonymous digital survey seeking their views on the team's strengths and areas requiring improvement. The responses signify a common sentiment: The team appreciates the flexible working hours but sees a gap in skills training. Using this feedback, you then initiate monthly skill-sharing sessions and workshops to upskill your team.

3. **Benchmark against industry best practices.** Compare your organization's performance and capabilities to your industry's best practices and standards to identify areas where you excel or need improvement. This valuable perspective on how your organization stacks up against the competition highlights potential areas for growth and innovation. Let's say that you manage an IT support team, and while the team's resolution rate is good, you wonder whether "good" is enough. You decide to attend industry conferences and webinars, and you explore leading research to understand best practices in IT support. Your findings reveal that while your team has a commendable first-call

resolution rate, leading companies have incorporated AI chatbots to handle initial queries to free up human agents for more complex issues. This realization motivates you to explore integrating AI-driven solutions to bolster your team's efficiency.

4. **Analyze past successes and failures.** Look back on your organization's history and examine successes and failures to glean valuable insights and lessons. Identifying patterns and trends can help you better understand your organization's strengths and weaknesses, thereby informing future strategies. Let's say that you're at the helm of a product launch team for a tech firm. Recognizing the importance of historical data, you organize retrospective meetings for each of the past five product launches. Delving into the intricacies of each campaign, you note that the products that underwent comprehensive beta-testing with real users were received better post-launch, and that the products pushed to market without substantial user testing had more post-launch issues. This informational gem motivates you to incorporate extensive user testing phases for all future products.

Innovation and Continuous Improvement

With your organization's strengths and weaknesses in hand, it's time to unleash your inner gardener by cultivating a fertile environment for innovation and continuous improvement. A culture of innovation is the lifeblood of any organization seeking to navigate the turbulent waters of change and disruption. It begins with a commitment to learning, experimentation, and growth.

Below are some considerations for cultivating a culture of ingenuity and constant betterment:

1. **Encourage a growth mindset.** Encourage a belief within your organization that talent and abilities are developed and enhanced through hard work, learning, and perseverance. By embracing this mindset, employees will be more likely to take risks, learn from mistakes, and embrace new challenges.

2. **Foster open communication and collaboration.** Create an environment where ideas and opinions can flow freely, and where employees feel comfortable sharing thoughts and suggestions without fear of judgment or reprisal. Promote collaboration and cross-functional teamwork, breaking down silos and promoting the exchange of ideas and perspectives.

3. **Celebrate creativity and experimentation.** Recognize and reward these essential qualities, even when they don't lead to immediate success. By celebrating the process of innovation and learning, you create a culture where employees are motivated to think outside the box and explore new ideas and possibilities.

4. **Provide resources and support for innovation.** Equip your employees with the tools, resources, and support they need to innovate and experiment, which might include training, technology, or funding. Create dedicated time and space for brainstorming, ideation, and prototyping.

5. **Implement a continuous improvement process.** Establish a systematic process for identifying, prioritizing, and implementing improvements, which could entail setting up regular feedback loops. Conduct performance reviews and use tools like lean methodologies or Six Sigma to drive continuous improvement.

The Netflix Evolution

Netflix has excelled at extracting internal capabilities and leveraging them for strategic advantage. Initially a DVD rental service, it recognized the potential of streaming technology and pivoted to become a leading provider of on-demand video content. The transition required a significant investment in technology, infrastructure, and content acquisition, all of which were successfully managed by Netflix's agile and innovative team.

A key element of its success has been the emphasis on cultivating a culture of innovation and continuous improvement. Employees are encouraged to experiment, learn from failures, and share insights with the rest of the organization. This has led to innovations such as the development of a proprietary recommendation algorithm that personalizes content suggestions for each user.

Netflix's ability to unearth and capitalize on its internal capabilities has allowed it to disrupt the traditional entertainment industry, establishing itself as a global leader in streaming content. By continually refining its platform and expanding its content library, the company has created a loyal and growing user base worldwide.

Leveraging Existing Resources and Assets

The final step in your treasure hunt is to harness your organization's hidden potential, leveraging your existing resources and assets for strategic advantage. Like a resourceful sleuth, you find creative ways to make the most of the tools at your disposal and to turn your organization's strengths and capabilities into a powerful engine for growth, innovation, and transformation.

Below are some action items for leveraging your existing resources and assets for strategic advantage.

1. **Identify and prioritize core capabilities.** Analyze your organization's strengths and resources, identifying those that are most critical to your strategic objectives and competitive advantage. Focus your efforts on nurturing and developing these key capabilities while also considering how they can be leveraged to create new opportunities to drive innovation.

2. **Maximize the value of your talent.** Unleash the full potential of your workforce. Ensure that employees are engaged, empowered, and equipped with the skills and resources they need to succeed. Invest in training and development, provide opportunities for career growth, and foster a culture of recognition and reward to maximize the value of your human capital.

3. **Optimize your processes and systems.** Streamline your organization's processes and systems to eliminate waste, reduce complexity, and improve efficiency. Use tools like process mapping, value stream analysis, and lean methodologies to identify areas for improvement, and implement changes that promote operational excellence.

4. **Leverage technology and data.** Harness the power of technology and data to drive innovation, improve decision making, and enhance your organization's capabilities. Explore emerging technologies like artificial intelligence, big data, and the Internet of Things. Consider how to integrate them into your strategy and operations to create a competitive edge.

5. **Foster strategic alliances and partnerships.** Look for opportunities to collaborate with external partners, suppliers, and customers to expand your organization's capabilities and resources. By pooling resources and expertise, you can create synergies that foster innovation, improve efficiency, and enhance your competitive position.

Extracting internal capabilities is a critical component of successful strategic leadership. By assessing organizational strengths and weaknesses, cultivating a culture of innovation and continuous improvement, and leveraging existing resources and assets for strategic advantage, you can unleash the hidden potential within your organization. Chart a bold course toward growth, innovation, and transformation.

Reflective Questions: Unearthing Hidden Potential

1. How can leaders assess their organization's strengths and weaknesses?

2. What are some ways to cultivate a culture of innovation and continuous improvement?

3. How can existing resources and assets be leveraged for strategic advantage?

4. What challenges might leaders face when trying to unearth hidden potential within their organization?

5. Can you think of an example of a time when your company successfully tapped into its internal capabilities to drive change?

6. How do you ensure that an organization's internal strengths are aligned with external market demands and opportunities?

7. In what ways can cross-functional collaboration contribute to uncovering and maximizing the latent potential within an organization?

6.
Establish Resource Allocation: Fueling the Engine of Change

Resource allocation isn't just pouring fuel into the engine—it's choosing the right octane for the race ahead.

— Christopher Meade, PhD

Financial, Human, and Technological Resources

Change leaders, start your engines. As you rev up for the rewarding race toward the checkered flag of growth, innovation, and transformation, it's essential to ensure that your organization has the right fuel to power your journey. Establishing resource allocation is like filling up your tank with the perfect blend of financial, human, and technological resources—all aligned with your strategic priorities to propel you toward success.

Here's how to align your resources with strategic priorities:

1. **Develop a strategic resource allocation plan.** Create a comprehensive plan outlining how your organization will allocate its financial, human, and technological resources to support your strategic objectives. This plan should be based on a thorough analysis of your organization's strengths, weaknesses, opportunities, and potential threats, as well as an understanding of the external context and competitive landscape.

2. **Prioritize investments based on impact and alignment.** Evaluate each potential investment or resource allocation

based on its expected impact on your strategic objectives. Is it aligned with your organization's mission, values, and competitive advantage? Focus on allocating resources to the areas with the highest potential for growth, innovation, and transformation.

3. **Involve key stakeholders in the decision-making process.** Engage key stakeholders, including employees, executives, and board members, in the resource-allocation process. Ensure buy-in and support for your strategic priorities to help create a shared sense of ownership and commitment to the organization's goals and objectives.

Balancing Short-Term and Long-Term Investments

As a change advocate, you've got a delicate balancing act: juggling your investments, both short- and long-term. Like the tightrope walker, you must maintain equilibrium. You need to ensure that your organization is both nimble enough to respond to immediate challenges and opportunities while also building the foundation for long-term success and sustainability.

Let's explore some tips for balancing short-term and long-term investments.

1. **Distinguish between them.** Clearly differentiate between short-term investments that address immediate needs or opportunities, and long-term investments that bolster your organization's future growth, innovation, and transformation. This distinction will help guide your resource-allocation decisions while ensuring that you maintain the right balance between the two.

2. **Allocate resources to both short-term and long-term priorities.** Earmark a portion of your resources for immediate needs and opportunities, and also dedicate some of them to

long-term investments that'll drive future growth, innovation, and transformation. This balanced approach will help ensure that you can seize opportunities in the short term while also building a foundation for the long haul.

3. **Monitor and adjust your resource allocation.** Regularly review and adjust your resource allocation to ensure that you're maintaining the right balance between the short term and long term. Use performance metrics, feedback from stakeholders, and changes in the external context to inform your decisions, ensuring that your resource allocation remains aligned with your strategic priorities.

SpaceX's Resourceful Ascent

SpaceX may be considered unique in many ways (reuse of thrusters, Mars focus, dozens of engines per vehicle, etc.), but it's largely been successful due to its strategic resource allocation. It's channeled significant portions of its revenue and investment back into R&D, understanding that long-term success in the space industry requires constant innovation (and change). This reinvestment strategy ensures that SpaceX remains on the cutting edge, as seen in its ambitious Starship project, which is aimed at interplanetary travel.

As for human resources, SpaceX remains a magnet for top worldwide talent. The company's clear vision and pioneering projects, such as the Mars colonization mission, appeal to those who are passionate about space and want to be a part of a groundbreaking vision. By aligning its hiring and talent development processes with its strategic objectives, SpaceX ensures that its workforce is always equipped and motivated to tackle the next big challenge.

Also, SpaceX's decision to develop much of its software and hardware in-house is a testament to its dedication to maintaining control over its technology. This enables quicker decision making, faster iterations and changes, and a seamless integration of technological components. When a specific technology doesn't exist or meet SpaceX's needs, the company creates it, ensuring that its technological resources are always in alignment with its goals.

The balance between short-term and long-term investments is a tightrope that SpaceX has mastered. While the company is invested in (very) long-term projects like the colonization of Mars, it also recognizes the need for current revenue streams and milestones. This led to its commercial satellite launches and contracts with NASA for cargo resupply missions to the ISS. These contracts provide consistent revenue, which, in turn, funds the company's ambitious, long-term projects.

SpaceX's development of the Falcon 1, Falcon 9, and Falcon Heavy rockets showcases this balance. While each version had long-term implications, they also served immediate market needs by generating revenue and establishing SpaceX's credibility in the space-launch industry.

Its Starlink project, which created a satellite-based internet service, is another prime example. While it promises to be a significant revenue generator in the short term, the project also aligns with Musk's vision for providing internet on Mars in the long term.

SpaceX's mastery in strategic resource allocation isn't merely about having vast resources but also about understanding where, when, and how to deploy them. The company's ability to synchronize its financial, human, and technological assets—all while balancing immediate needs with futuristic vision—sets it apart in the aerospace industry.

Agility and Flexibility in Resource Allocation

In today's fast-paced and ever-changing business landscape, agility and flexibility are the name of the game. As a change influencer, you must adapt and pivot. Be ready, willing, and able to reallocate resources as needed to respond to new challenges and opportunities that emerge.

Let's look at how to ensure agility and flexibility in your resource allocation.

1. **Build flexibility into your resource-allocation plan.** Set aside a portion of your budget, time, and other resources for unexpected opportunities or challenges. This allows you to respond quickly and effectively when the need arises, without sacrificing strategic priorities. For example, as a manager overseeing a project, you could allocate 90% of your budget to well-defined tasks and expenses while wisely reserving the remaining 10% as a contingency fund. When an unexpected software upgrade is needed midway through the project, you're prepared. You can tap into this reserve without derailing the main objectives, ensuring that the project stays on track and within budget.

2. **Encourage a culture of adaptability.** Promote a growth mindset, establish open communication, and foster a willingness to embrace change. Encourage employees to be open to new ideas, to learn from failures, and to adapt different approaches. This adaptable culture creates an environment where your organization can respond effectively to changes in the external context and seize emerging opportunities. Let's say that you're the leader of a sales team, and you notice that traditional sales methods are yielding diminishing returns. Rather than resisting change, you organize brainstorming sessions and encourage team members to explore innovative sales techniques. When one of your team members proposes a new approach based on social media engagement, you support it. This adaptability leads to an uptick in sales and introduces a new, effective strategy to your repertoire.

3. **Establish a process for reallocating resources.** Develop a systematic process for repositioning resources in response to changing circumstances, new opportunities, or shifts in strategic priorities. This might mean setting up regular checkpoints or reviews to assess the effectiveness of your resource allocation. Gather feedback from stakeholders and adjust your approach. If you're the head of a marketing department, you could hold monthly reviews with your team to assess ongoing campaigns. When you discover that one campaign is underperforming, you can solicit feedback and decide to redirect funds to a more promising initiative. This regular review system ensures that your marketing budget aligns with the most impactful projects.

4. **Maintain a strong focus on results and impact.** Use performance metrics and indicators to track progress and inform decision making. By maintaining a strong focus on results, you can make agile and informed decisions about reallocating resources in response to changes in the external context or emerging opportunities. Let's say that you're managing a product-development team. Rather than merely tracking the number of features being added, you should also give importance to user feedback and the actual impact of the features. When you find that a recently added feature isn't resonating with users, you can reallocate resources to refine it based on user feedback, ensuring that your team's efforts yield meaningful results.

5. **Foster cross-functional collaboration.** Encourage collaboration and communication across functions and departments, and facilitate the efficient and effective allocation of resources. Break down silos and foster a culture of cooperation so that your organization will be positioned to respond to new challenges and opportunities. Reallocate resources as needed to drive growth, innovation, and transformation. For instance, in your role as a manager at a manufacturing

firm, you might notice how a communication gap between the design and production teams is leading to inefficiencies. You could introduce joint weekly meetings and collaborative workshops to bridge the gap. As the teams begin to collaborate, they'll share insights, refine processes, and effectively allocate resources to optimize the manufacturing process to drive growth and innovation.

Establishing resource allocation is a vital component of successful change-driven leadership. By aligning financial, human, and technological resources with strategic priorities, balancing short-term and long-term investments, and ensuring agility and flexibility in resource allocation, you'll fuel the engine of change and set your organization on a rewarding course toward growth, innovation, and transformation.

Reflective Questions: Establishing Resource Allocation

1. How can leaders align financial, human, and technological resources with strategic priorities?

2. What are the challenges you've encountered in balancing short-term and long-term investments in a change initiative?

3. Why is it important to ensure agility and flexibility in resource allocation?

4. How can leaders make tough decisions about resource allocation during times of change?

5. Can you think of an example of a time when your company successfully allocated resources to drive change?

6. How does the culture of an organization influence its approach to resource allocation?

7. In what ways can cross-functional collaboration enhance the effectiveness of resource allocation during transformative periods?

7.
Execute Strategic Action: Translating Vision into Reality

In the kitchen of transformation, vision sets the table and strategy crafts the recipe, but relentless execution is the flame that turns aspirations into a gourmet reality.

— Christopher Meade, PhD

A Comprehensive and Actionable Change Roadmap

Change drivers, it's time to roll up your sleeves and dive into the nitty-gritty of executing a strategic plan. Your audacious vision for change and your well-aligned resources are like the ingredients of a mouthwatering recipe. Let's blend them together, fire up the stove, and cook up a feast of growth, innovation, and transformation. Developing a comprehensive and actionable change roadmap is the key to translating your vision into action and making your strategic plan a glorious reality.

Here's how to create a change roadmap that'll guide your organization on its journey:

Break down strategic objectives into actionable steps. Smaller, more-manageable steps or milestones can be tackled in a logical and sequential manner, making your change roadmap more actionable and clearer. This helps your organization to focus on the specific tasks and activities required to achieve your strategic objectives.

Assign roles and responsibilities. Clearly define the roles and responsibilities of each team member, department, or function involved in executing the strategic plan. This helps ensure accountability and ownership, as well as foster collaboration and coordination across the organization.

Set realistic timelines and deadlines. Establish reasonable expectations for each step or milestone on your change roadmap. Consider the complexity of the tasks, the availability of resources, and the need for flexibility in response to changing circumstances. This helps keep your organization focused on achieving its strategic objectives.

Develop a communication plan. Create a communication strategy to keep stakeholders informed of your progress, to celebrate successes, and to address any challenges or setbacks that arise. This helps maintain momentum, engagement, and support for your change initiatives.

Focus and Discipline

With your change roadmap in hand, it's time to hit the ground running and start implementing your initiatives with focus and discipline. Like a skilled gardener, you'll need to carefully sow the seeds of change, nurture them with patience and care, and ensure that they have the right conditions to grow and flourish.

Below are some strategies for implementing your change initiatives:

1. **Start with quick wins.** Kick off your change initiatives with a few quick wins—small, high-impact projects that can be completed relatively quickly and generate immediate results. This helps build momentum and enthusiasm for your change efforts, demonstrating the value of your strategic plan.

2. **Maintain a focus on your strategic objectives.** Stay laser-focused on your strategic objectives to ensure that all initiatives are aligned with and contribute to their realization. This helps maintain a sense of purpose and direction, ensuring that your change efforts are focused on what truly matters.

3. **Establish routines and rituals to support change.** Create regular progress meetings, performance tracking, and celebrations of success that support the implementation of your change initiatives. These routines and rituals help embed change into your organization's culture, and they also create a sense of continuity and commitment.

4. **Empower your team to take ownership.** Give your team the autonomy and resources they need to succeed. This helps create a sense of accountability, ownership, and responsibility, and it also fosters a culture of innovation and continuous improvement.

Southwest's Flight to Democratize the Skies

Southwest Airlines broke molds and paradigms in the airline industry in the 1970s, taking aviation "to the people" and becoming a beacon of translating vision into reality. Starting with a humble vision of providing affordable air travel, Southwest emerged as a trailblazer—a gamechanger—as a budget airline and in the entire aviation sector. Its vision wasn't merely about affordable prices—it set out to democratize the skies. And it *did* that.

It had a bold plan to overhaul the traditional aviation model. The primary objectives were clear—quick turnaround times, a fleet composed of only one type of aircraft for ease of maintenance, and a no-frills approach. The action plan entailed serious cost savings while ensuring that the passenger experience was never compromised. It's not an easy thing to do to save money *and* make people happy.

But Southwest's management broke down the overall mission into smaller actionable objectives, such as introducing a point-to-point flight system instead of the traditional hub-and-spoke model. This reduced costs and improved efficiency. The simplicity of this plan made it actionable—every task, whether it was faster boarding processes or staff multitasking, had a defined purpose.

Southwest even expanded on the concept of clearly defined roles. Pilots assisted with baggage, and flight attendants helped tidy the plane for the next journey. This sense of teamwork, coupled with clarity in roles, ensured that every member was accountable and that the entire process was streamlined. Its culture of open communication meant that everyone—from the pilots to the ground crew—was on the same page. Regular briefings ensured that the entire team was aligned with the company's strategic priorities.

Execution became a core strength and marketing triumph. Quick wins, like industry-leading turnaround times, garnered attention. Its focus remained razor-sharp, sticking to its primary routes and avoiding the lure of international expansions that could dilute its operating model. Rituals like its unique way of making in-flight announcements fostered a culture that was distinctly Southwest, setting the airline apart from its counterparts. It gave it something most corporations lack—a personality. How about that for turning vision into reality?

Southwest's prowess lies not just in its strategic planning but also in the impeccable execution of that strategy. It took a comprehensive vision, broke it down into tangible actions, and then set about methodically making it a reality. The airline's commitment to its strategic imperatives is a testament to the power of disciplined and focused execution in the corporate world.

Monitoring Progress and Adjusting Course

As you navigate the twists and turns of your change journey, it's essential to keep a watchful eye on your progress, monitoring achievements and adjusting course as needed. Like a seasoned sailor, you'll need to read the winds and currents, adjusting course to ensure that you stay on track and reach your destination.

Let's look at some suggestions for monitoring progress and adjusting your course.

1. **Establish performance metrics and indicators.** Develop a set of metrics and indicators that help measure the performance, progress, and impact of your change initiatives. These metrics should closely align with your strategic objectives, and they should provide clear, quantifiable evidence of your organization's progress toward achieving its goals. It's important to choose the right yardstick by setting metrics that echo your vision, like setting up monthly customer-satisfaction scores to mirror your objective of enhancing user experience.

2. **Conduct regular progress reviews.** Schedule regular progress reviews to assess the status of your change initiatives, using your performance metrics and indicators as a guide. These reviews help identify successes, challenges, and areas for improvement. Ensure that your organization remains focused on its strategic objectives. You might consider marking your calendar for monthly strategy check-ins, ensuring that your path aligns with the map you've drawn for success.

3. **Be prepared to adapt and pivot.** Recognizing that change is an inherently unpredictable and dynamic process, be prepared to adjust your change initiatives in response to new information, changing circumstances, or unforeseen challenges. This flexibility helps ensure that your organiza-

tion remains nimble and responsive in the face of change. Imagine a situation where a sudden market shift sends ripples your way, and you're ready to shift your sails and recalibrate, ensuring that you're not blown off course.

4. **Learn from setbacks and failures.** Embrace obstacles and hindrances as opportunities for learning and growth. Analyze what went wrong, identify the root causes, and apply these insights to improve your change initiatives. This helps create a culture of continuous improvement and resilience within your organization. If a project stumbles, you don't just brush it off—you dissect the fall, uncover the lesson, and ensure that your next step is on firmer ground.

5. **Celebrate successes and milestones.** Take the time to celebrate your organization's triumphs by recognizing and rewarding the hard work and achievements of your team members. These celebrations help maintain morale, engagement, and momentum, and they remind everyone of the purpose and value of your change efforts. When a goal is reached, throw a small office party or hand out achievement badges. Make sure that each victory, no matter how small, gets its moment in the sun.

Executing a strategic plan is the linchpin of dynamic leadership. By developing a comprehensive and actionable change roadmap, implementing change initiatives with focus and discipline, and monitoring progress and adjusting your course as needed, you'll translate your vision into action—and, ultimately, reality. This helps propel your organization toward growth, innovation, and transformation.

Reflective Questions: Executing a Strategic Plan

1. What are the key components of a comprehensive and action-able change roadmap?

2. How can leaders implement change initiatives with focus and discipline?

3. Why is it important to monitor progress and adjust course as needed during the change process?

4. What challenges might leaders face when executing a strategic plan?

5. Can you think of an example of a time when a company successfully executed a strategic plan to drive change?

6. How do you ensure that every team member understands their role and responsibility in the execution of your strategic plan?

7. In what ways can leaders cultivate a culture of resilience and adaptability during the process of executing strategic changes?

8.
Encourage the Heart:
Igniting Passion and Commitment

In the orchestra of change, a leader's heart is
the baton that ignites the passion, rhythm, and
commitment of every player.

— Christopher Meade, PhD

An Urgency and Excitement for Change

It's time to fan the flames of passion and commitment toward change within your organization, and to fire up a burning desire for innovation, transformation, and growth. Encouraging the heart is all about tapping into the emotional energy of your team members, as well as creating a sense of urgency and excitement for change that'll propel them and the organization forward with unstoppable momentum.

Below are some recommendations for creating a sense of urgency and excitement for change.

1. **Share a compelling story.** Craft an intriguing narrative that eloquently communicates the importance and urgency of your change initiatives. Use vivid language and emotive storytelling to paint a vivid picture of the challenges, opportunities, and potential rewards at stake. This helps engage your team members' hearts and minds, and it creates a sense of urgency and excitement for change.

2. **Highlight the benefits of change.** Clearly articulate the benefits of your change initiatives, for both the organiza-

tion and individual team members. By highlighting the potential rewards and positive outcomes of change, you'll inspire your team to embrace the change journey and commit to its success.

3. **Create a sense of shared ownership.** Foster a feeling of shared ownership and responsibility for the success of your change initiatives. Involve your team members in decision-making and problem-solving processes. This helps create a sense of collective purpose and commitment, generating excitement for the change journey ahead.

Recognizing and Rewarding Change Champions

Change champions are too often the unsung heroes of an organization, and it's time to change that. They work tirelessly behind the scenes to drive growth, innovation, and transformation, and so recognizing and rewarding these change champions is essential for encouraging the heart. It demonstrates your appreciation for their efforts and helps to build a culture of commitment and accountability. Seeing good people lauded and celebrated emboldens all good people's hearts.

Let's examine some ways to recognize and reward your change champions.

1. **Celebrate their achievements.** Take the time to publicly acknowledge and celebrate the achievements of your change champions. Highlight the specific impact of their efforts on the success of your change initiatives, as this helps reinforce the importance of their work and inspires others to follow in their footsteps. Envision a situation where at the next company webinar, you highlight a team member's ingenious marketing tactic that boosted your rebranding campaign.

2. **Provide opportunities for growth and development.** Offer your change champions opportunities for personal and professional growth, such as training programs, mentorship, or stretch assignments. This not only rewards their efforts but also helps to build their skills and capabilities, further enhancing their ability to drive change within your organization. Consider offering a colleague a spot in your leadership training as a nod to their stellar performance on the change task force.

3. **Foster a culture of recognition and appreciation.** Create a culture where recognizing and appreciating your team are the norm. Encourage team members to celebrate one another's successes, and express gratitude for each other's contributions. This helps create a positive and supportive work environment, where change champions feel valued and appreciated. For example, you could kick off every team meeting with a five-minute shout-out, allowing peers to highlight a colleague's outstanding contribution.

Communicating Progress and Celebrating Milestones

As your organization embarks on its change journey, be sure to keep team members informed on progress and to celebrate milestones and achievements. This not only maintains momentum and enthusiasm for your change initiatives—it also serves as a powerful reminder of the value and impact of your efforts.

Below are some tips for communicating progress and celebrating milestones:

1. **Establish regular communication channels.** Share updates on your change initiatives via newsletters, progress reports, or team meetings. This helps ensure that your team

members stay informed and engaged, and also that they feel connected to the change journey.

2. **Be transparent and honest.** Communicate your progress and challenges openly and honestly, sharing both your successes and setbacks. This transparency helps build trust and credibility, and it also demonstrates your commitment to learning and growth.

3. **Create opportunities for celebration.** Organize events and activities to celebrate the milestones and achievements of your change initiatives, such as team lunches, award ceremonies, or social gatherings. These celebrations help foster a sense of camaraderie and pride, reminding your team members of the importance and value of their efforts.

4. **Share stories of success.** Collect and share success stories from your change initiatives. Highlight the impact and benefits of your efforts on individuals, teams, and the organization, as these stories help inspire and motivate your team members while serving as powerful examples of the power of change.

5. **Encourage team members to share their experiences.** Create opportunities for your team members to share their insights and experiences from the change journey, such as through presentations, workshops, or informal discussions. This helps foster a sense of shared learning and growth, and it creates a stronger sense of connection and commitment to the change process.

Patagonia's Passion-Packed Pursuit

Outdoor clothing and gear company Patagonia is renowned for its passionate commitment to environmental and social causes. Founder Yvon Chouinard has instilled a sense of urgency and excitement for change within the company, driving a culture that prioritizes sustainability and corporate responsibility.

The company encourages the heart by regularly recognizing and rewarding employees who champion its mission, values, and initiatives. It also communicates progress and celebrates milestones—such as reaching 100% renewable energy at its headquarters—to keep employees engaged and motivated.

True to the spirit of encouraging the heart, Patagonia has taken steps that few corporations dare to—or even *care* to, unfortunately. It's championed programs allowing employees to engage in paid environmental internships, promoted grassroots activism, and nurtured a sense of community with on-site childcare—all girded by a genuine care for its people and the planet. Its "Worn Wear" program, an anthem to sustainability, motivates customers to breathe new life into old gear rather than discard and replace.

By fostering a culture of passion and commitment to its mission, Patagonia has not only created a loyal workforce but also inspired a devoted customer base that shares and celebrates its values. This has greatly contributed to the company's ongoing success and growth in the competitive outdoor clothing industry.

Encouraging the heart is a vital element of successful change-focused leadership. It helps to ignite passion and commitment within your organization, creating a powerful engine for growth, innovation, and transformation. By creating a sense of urgency and excitement for change, recognizing and rewarding change champions, and communicating progress and celebrating milestones, you fan the flames of passion and commitment, helping to propel your organization toward a brighter and bolder future.

Reflective Questions: Encouraging the Heart

1. Why is it important to create a sense of urgency and excitement for change?

2. How can leaders recognize and reward change champions within their organization?

3. What are some effective ways to communicate progress and celebrate milestones during a change initiative?

4. How does encouraging the heart contribute to the success of a change initiative?

5. Can you think of an example of a time when a leader effectively encouraged the heart and inspired passion and commitment in others?

6. In what ways have you personally felt the impact of leadership that encouraged the heart in your professional journey?

7. How can you integrate more heart-centered practices into your leadership approach moving forward?

9.
Evaluate Results:
Assessing the Impact of Change

Like a detective with a magnifying glass, in the world of enterprise, we use data to zoom in on the details, discern patterns, and crack the code to future successes.

— Christopher Meade, PhD

Success Metrics and Indicators

Change drivers, it's time to put on your data-driven detective hats and investigate the impact of your change initiatives. Evaluating results is a crucial element of successful growth-focused leadership, ensuring that your organization is on the right track and making the necessary adjustments to drive continuous improvement.

To kick off our evaluation journey, we must establish clear success metrics and indicators that'll help measure the progress and impact of our change initiatives. These metrics should align with strategic objectives and provide clear, quantifiable evidence of the organization's progress toward achieving its goals.

Let's explore some strategies for establishing clear success metrics and indicators.

1. **Identify key performance indicators (KPIs).** Determine the KPIs that best capture the success of your change initiatives. Focus on those that are directly related to your strategic objectives and most meaningful to your organization.

2. **Set specific, measurable, achievable, relevant, and time-bound (SMART) goals.** When establishing your success metrics, ensure that they're SMART so that your metrics are clear, actionable, and meaningful. This enables you to track your progress more effectively.

3. **Align metrics with stakeholder expectations.** Your success metrics and indicators should reflect the expectations of key stakeholders, such as customers, employees, and shareholders. This ensures that your evaluation efforts are focused on what truly matters to your organization.

Regular Performance Reviews and Feedback Loops

Once you've established your success metrics and indicators, you can now conduct regular performance reviews and feedback loops to assess the progress and impact of your change initiatives. These reviews will help you identify successes, challenges, and areas for improvement, ensuring that your organization remains focused on its strategic objectives.

Below are some suggestions for conducting regular performance reviews and feedback loops.

1. **Schedule regular progress reviews.** These reviews must be frequent enough to provide timely insights and feedback, but not so frequent as to become burdensome or disruptive.

2. **Use a consistent evaluation framework.** Develop a consistent (and objective) evaluation procedure that can be used to assess the progress and impact of your change initiatives. Ensure that your performance reviews are systematic, rigorous, and comparable across different initiatives.

3. **Gather feedback from multiple sources.** Input and feedback should be collected from a range of key players, such as team members, stakeholders, customers, and partners. This will ensure that you're gaining a more comprehensive and nuanced understanding of your initiatives' progress and impact.

4. **Foster a culture of open and honest feedback.** Create a safe space for constructive criticism and learning that encourages your team members to contribute their thoughts on the progress and impact of your change initiatives.

Learning from Successes and Failures

The final piece of the evaluation puzzle is learning from what works and what doesn't. These insights can support your drive for ongoing improvement and finetune your change initiatives. Embrace both your triumphs and your setbacks as valuable learning opportunities, and use them to fuel your organization's ongoing growth, innovation, and transformation.

Let's examine some recommendations for learning from successes and failures.

1. **Conduct a root cause analysis.** When evaluating the results of your change initiatives, conduct a root cause analysis to identify the underlying factors contributing to your successes and failures. This helps you pinpoint the key drivers of your performance and identify areas for improvement. If, for example, you notice a dip in sales, you can dig deeper and discover that a recent marketing strategy wasn't resonating with your target audience.

2. **Share your learning across the organization.** Confirm to your team members that they can benefit from the collective experiences and apply lessons to their own work.

For instance, following a successful project completion, you could organize a team meeting to share lessons learned from what worked and what didn't to use for future projects.

3. **Implement a continuous improvement mindset.** Encourage your team members to constantly seek opportunities for learning, growth, and innovation. This helps create a culture of adaptability and resilience, and it enables your organization to thrive in the face of change. For example, every time a project concludes, you could encourage your team to brainstorm ways they could perform even better next time.

4. **Celebrate learning and growth.** Reinforce and recognize the importance of continuous improvement and learning that comes from both successes and failures. This helps create a positive and supportive work environment where team members feel empowered to take risks and learn from their experiences. For instance, at the end of each quarter, you could host a companywide event highlighting both the triumphs and challenges faced, emphasizing the learning from each.

5. **Adjust your strategies and plans as needed.** Use your evaluation insights and learning to finetune your strategies and plans. Ensure that your change initiatives remain aligned with your strategic objectives and focused on driving meaningful results. This helps guarantee that your organization remains agile and responsive to the ever-changing business landscape. Imagine a situation where, after reviewing last month's performance data, you decide to tweak the customer service protocol to address the rising customer complaints.

Toyota's Evolution Engine

Toyota is famous for change, for evolution of products, and for being at the vanguard of metric analysis and new ideas. The multinational automotive manufacturer doesn't just assemble cars—it weaves a rich tapestry of continuous improvement, data-driven decisions, and actionable feedback. The celebrated "Toyota Production System," which emphasizes the elimination of waste, inefficiency, and inconsistency, showcases the company's meticulous attention to detail in evaluating results.

Every bolt-tightened and every component installed has a metric behind it, a purpose. Toyota's commitment to *"genchi genbutsu"*—which translates to "go and see"—demonstrates its belief in understanding problems firsthand. Instead of relying on second-hand reports, leaders venture onto their production floors, understand the nuances, and make decisions based on direct observation.

The culture also fosters open communication, as employees at all levels are being encouraged to voice concerns and propose improvements. This grassroots feedback system ensures that potential pitfalls are addressed before they escalate into problematic issues and that innovative ideas are continually infused into the process.

The automaker's capacity to pivot based on these processes has led to breakthroughs like the hybrid technology in the Prius, or the hydrogen fuel-cell technology in the Mirai. These aren't just cars—they're testaments to Toyota's unwavering commitment to evaluate, adapt, and evolve.

For Toyota, evaluating results isn't just a post-mortem task—it's a living philosophy that runs through the DNA of every process, every employee, and every car. For leaders aspiring to drive change, Toyota's legacy offers a roadmap—a journey where each milestone is an opportunity for reflection, learning, and recalibration. Embracing this approach ensures that the company doesn't merely survive but rather thrives in an ever-evolving global landscape.

Reflective Questions: Evaluating Results

1. Why is it important to establish clear success metrics and indicators for change initiatives?

2. How can leaders conduct regular performance reviews and create feedback loops during a change process?

3. What role does learning from successes and failures play in driving continuous improvement?

4. How can leaders ensure that they're objectively evaluating the results of change initiatives?

5. Can you think of an example of a company that effectively evaluated the results of a change initiative and used those insights to improve?

6. In what ways has your organization incorporated a culture of continuous improvement, and how has it benefited from it?

7. How do you differentiate between a setback that's a part of the learning process and one that indicates a fundamental flaw in the initiative?

10.
Evolutionary Process: Sustaining Change and Momentum

Just as a river constantly reshapes its course, businesses must embrace continuous learning and innovation to ensure that they flow seamlessly into tomorrow's opportunities.

— Christopher Meade, PhD

Continuous Learning and Adaptation

Welcome to the grand finale of our celebration and implementation of change leadership. Now it's time to explore the evolutionary process of sustaining change and momentum, which ensures that your organization can remain nimble, adaptable, and ready to tackle whatever challenges and opportunities lie ahead.

The first step in the evolutionary process is fostering a culture of continuous learning and adaptation. In today's ever-changing business landscape, organizations that fail to adapt and learn are destined for the metaphorical dustbin of history. So, change leaders, let's go forth and cultivate a culture of perpetual growth and transformation.

Let's look at some great ideas for fostering a culture of continuous learning and adaptation.

1. **Encourage curiosity and questioning.** Create an environment where curiosity and questioning are celebrated. Foster a culture where team members are encouraged to

challenge the status quo, explore new ideas, and learn from experiences.

2. **Provide opportunities for learning and development.** Offer a variety of learning and development opportunities, such as workshops, seminars, and online courses, to help your team members expand their skills, knowledge, and capabilities.

3. **Embrace and learn from failure.** Encourage team members to view failure as a natural part of the learning process and an opportunity for growth and improvement. This helps to create a culture that values risk taking and experimentation, allowing team members to feel empowered to innovate and push the boundaries of what's possible.

Change and Innovation in the Organizational DNA

The next step in the evolutionary process is embedding change and innovation into the very fabric of your organization, making them integral components of your DNA. By doing so, you ensure that change and innovation become second nature to your team members to enable your organization to adapt with grace, acumen, and agility.

Below are some considerations for embedding change and innovation into organizational DNA:

1. **Align your organizational values and culture with change and innovation.** Stress the importance of adaptability, creativity, and perpetual improvement to ensure that the principles of innovation and change are interwoven into your team's values.

2. **Integrate change and innovation into your organizational systems and processes.** This can be done via per-

formance management, decision making, and strategic planning, and it assures that change and innovation are consistently reinforced and prioritized.

3. **Develop change and innovation competencies.** Your team members need these competencies in order to succeed, so ensure that you provide targeted training and development opportunities to help them build their skills.

Adobe: From Pixels to Evolutionary Progress

Fifty years ago, when people heard the word "adobe," images of mud huts often sprang to mind. But not anymore, as Adobe is now emblematic of digital adaptability and transformation. Venturing from its origins as a pioneering software provider, Adobe took a daring leap into the cloud realm with a subscription-based model. While initial responses were tepid, Adobe's commitment to listening, iterating, and continuously enhancing its suite ensured its emergence as an industry mainstay.

Adobe promotes a culture of continuous innovation. Its hackathons and the "Red Box Program" are symbolic of an ethos that values employee-driven creativity and forward thinking. These initiatives not only foster a culture of continuous growth but have also resulted in product enhancements and novel features.

Further fortifying its position in the marketplace, Adobe makes strategic acquisitions, like those of Magento and Marketo, signifying its pulse on the evolving digital landscape. These moves not only diversify Adobe's offerings—they anticipate the future needs of the digital marketing domain.

The company's certification renewals and frequent "Future of Work" report releases exhibit its dedication to staying at the forefront of industry trends and equipping its community for the same.

Adobe's journey reflects its genius in navigating the digital evolution—and revolution. Seamlessly blending its current strategies with a vision for the future, it encapsulates the essence of evolutionary brilliance in the tech arena.

Preparing for Future Disruptions and Opportunities

The final piece of the evolutionary puzzle comes down to verifying that your organization remains poised to seize the moment and capitalize on emerging trends and shifts in the business landscape.

Below are some best practices for preparing for future disruptions and opportunities.

1. **Stay informed and anticipate change.** Keep your finger on the pulse of emerging trends, technologies, and developments in your industry. Anticipate how these shifts may impact your organization and its competitive landscape. For example, sign up for industry-specific webinars and conferences, ensuring that you're always clued into the latest market shifts.

2. **Foster strategic agility.** Ensure that your organization can quickly and effectively adapt to changing circumstances. Seize new opportunities, and navigate the complex and uncertain waters of the business world. You might consider initiating a monthly brainstorming session with your team to discuss and swiftly adapt to unforeseen challenges and opportunities.

3. **Encourage scenario planning and foresight exercises.** Explore potential future scenarios and their implications for your organization. This will help to broaden your strategic horizons and prepare you for a range of possible futures. For instance, you can schedule quarterly workshops

to roleplay various scenarios, helping your team visualize and prepare for potential outcomes.

The evolutionary process of sustaining change and momentum is a critical element of successful change-driven leadership. It fuels your organization to remain adaptable, resilient, and ready to tackle oncoming challenges and opportunities. By fostering a culture of continuous learning and adaptation, embedding change and innovation into your organizational DNA, and preparing for future disruptions and opportunities, you place your organization on a path of ongoing growth, innovation, and transformation.

Reflective Questions: Sustaining Change and Momentum

1. How can leaders foster a culture of continuous learning and adaptation within their organization?

2. What are some ways to embed change and innovation into an organization's DNA?

3. How can leaders prepare for future disruptions and opportunities in their industry?

4. What challenges might leaders face when trying to sustain change and momentum?

5. Can you think of an example of a company that successfully sustained change and momentum?

6. How do you measure the success of sustained change and innovation within your organization?

7. How can leaders ensure that the drive for change and innovation remains consistent and doesn't wane?

Final Thoughts

Leadership ignites the flame, change fuels the fire, and innovation sculpts the vision. Guided by the 10 Es, we construct the bridge to a brighter, transformed tomorrow.

— Christopher Meade, PhD

Reflecting on the Journey of Change Leadership

We've reached the end of our journey through the realm of change leadership, in which we've explored the peaks and valleys of strategic change, innovation, and transformation. As we pause to catch our breath and reflect on the adventure, let's take stock of the insights we've gleaned along the way.

We've explored the 10 Elements of Successful Change Leadership—from embracing change and envisioning the future to evaluating results and navigating the ever-evolving process of sustaining change and momentum. We've encountered helpful tools, strategies, and mindsets that equip us to tackle the challenges and opportunities that lie ahead. This information will empower us anew to lead our organizations to new heights of success and impact.

As we stand at the summit of our transformational leadership journey, we can look back at the path we've forged and the progress we've made. And we must always remember that organizational change isn't a one-time endeavor—it's an ongoing (and exciting) adventure. It's a continuous quest for learning, growth, and transformation that carries us thoughtfully forward into the unknown realms of the future.

Importance of Adaptability and Resilience

In today's rapidly changing business landscape, adaptability and resilience have emerged as the twin pillars of success. They enable us to thrive in the face of change, uncertainty, and disruption. As change champions, it's our responsibility to not only embody these qualities ourselves but also to instill them in our organizations. To be successful, we must cultivate a culture of agility, innovation, and continuous improvement.

By embracing adaptability and resilience, we ensure that our organizations remain nimble, responsive, and ready to seize the moment. Carpe diem! We prepare that moment to capitalize on emerging trends, technologies, and opportunities. We architect it to be able to navigate the complex and uncertain waters of the business world with grace, skill, and determination.

As we forge ahead into the boundless future, let's hold fast to the lessons we've learned and the insights we've gained. Let's use them as our compass and guide as we navigate the ever-changing seas of strategic change, innovation, and transformation.

Leaders of Change, Embrace It ALL

As we embark on the next season of our growth-oriented journey, let's embrace the challenge and opportunity that lie before us. The power of leading strategic change, innovation, and transformation is all at once exhilarating, empowering, and transformative.

It's not something to be feared or resisted—it's an opportunity for renewal and reinvention. It's a chance to break free from the shackles of the status quo and chart a bold new course toward a brighter, more prosperous, and more fulfilling future.

As change leaders, it's our mission and our privilege to be the catalysts, the visionaries, and the trailblazers who lead our organizations into an era of innovation, impact, and success. By embracing the challenge and opportunity of change, we unlock the full potential of our organizations, our teams, and ourselves. We make a lasting and meaningful difference. Is there anything greater in our work? I certainly think not.

So let's go forth with courage, conviction, and passion. Yes, let's seize the day—for the future is ours to shape, mold, and birth. The power to transform the world lies within our grasp. As the architects and the builders of the future, we rise to the challenge. As we embrace the opportunity to lead strategic change, innovation, and transformation, we'll leave an indelible mark on the world around us.

I would like to now offer a heartfelt word of encouragement and appreciation to all you change agents who dare to dream big, challenge the status quo, and strive to make a lasting, positive impact on the world. Your passion, determination, and commitment to growth and transformation are truly inspiring. It's an honor to be one of you—and to be *with* you on this challenging but immensely satisfying journey.

As we part ways and embark on our individual paths toward growth-centered leadership, let's proudly carry the lessons we've learned. May we continue to learn from one another, challenge one another, and inspire one another to reach ever-greater heights of achievement.

Let's raise a toast to the change architects of the world—the courageous, passionate trailblazers who dare to step into the unknown and shape a better future. May your journey be filled with adventure, growth, and success, and may you continue to forge a path of transformation, leaving a legacy of lasting change in your wake.

Onward, change leaders. The future awaits. Embrace the challenge and opportunity of leading strategic transformation. Let your light shine unabashedly bright, guiding the way for others to follow in your footsteps. May you tackle whatever challenges and opportunities the future holds—and may you emerge stronger, wiser, and more resilient than ever before.

Your organization and community need your vision, your passion, and your fearless spirit now more than ever. Together, let's create a brighter, more innovative, and more just future for all—one shaped by the transformative power of change and brought to life by the tenacious and indomitable spirit of change leaders like you.

Reflective Questions: Leading Change and Transformation

1. What are some key takeaways from the journey of change leadership presented in this book?

2. How has your understanding of adaptability and resilience evolved after reading?

3. What challenges and opportunities do you anticipate in leading strategic change, innovation, and transformation in your organization?

4. How will you apply the lessons learned from the 10 Elements of Successful Change Leadership in your personal or professional life?

5. Which of the elements resonated most with you, and why?

6. How can you inspire and motivate your team to embrace the principles of strategic change and innovation on a daily basis?

7. In what ways can you foster a culture that not only accepts but also actively seeks out continuous improvement and transformation within your organization?

10 Case Studies: Applying the 10 Elements of Change

Case Study 1: Embrace Change

Netflix's Shift from DVD Rentals to Streaming

Overview: Netflix's journey from a DVD rental service to a streaming giant illustrates the importance of embracing change in the face of industry disruption. In this case study, we delve deeper into the background, solutions, and results of Netflix's transition. We provide an account of how the company successfully navigated the rapidly shifting landscape of the entertainment industry.

Background: By the late 2000s, Netflix dominated the DVD rental market with its innovative mail-order service. However, as high-speed internet became more widely accessible, consumer preferences shifted toward streaming content online. Recognizing the impending decline of physical media, Netflix's leadership faced the challenge of adapting their business model to remain competitive in the rapidly evolving entertainment landscape.

Solutions:

1. **Strategic vision:** Netflix's leadership, led by CEO Reed Hastings, anticipated the rise of streaming and envisioned a future where the company would become a major player in the online entertainment space. This clear strategic vision allowed Netflix to stay ahead of the curve and transition from a DVD rental service to a streaming platform.

2. **Investment in technology:** With its vision set in stone, Netflix invested heavily in the development of streaming technology. This ensured that it could provide high-quality

content to users with minimal buffering and latency. The focus on technological innovation allowed the company to offer a superior streaming experience, which set it apart from competitors and attracted more subscribers.

3. **Content strategy:** As streaming became the primary focus of its business, the company adopted a two-pronged content strategy—acquiring licenses for popular movies and TV shows from studios, and then developing original content. This approach allowed Netflix to offer a diverse and compelling library of content that appealed to a wide range of audiences.

4. **Adaptive pricing and a subscription model:** Netflix stayed nimble and adapted its pricing and subscription model to accommodate the shift to streaming services. It offered customers flexible plans that provided unlimited streaming for a fixed monthly fee. This approach allowed the company to cater to the evolving needs and preferences of its user base.

Results:

1. **Rapid subscriber growth:** Netflix's transition to a streaming platform led to exponential growth of subscribers, as more and more consumers turned to online entertainment options. It eventually boasted over 200 million subscribers worldwide, making it one of the largest streaming services in the world.

2. **Global expansion:** The company's shift to streaming allowed it to greatly expand its reach beyond the United States, offering services to customers in over 190 countries. This global presence has contributed significantly to Netflix's success by diversifying its revenue streams and growing market share.

3. **Original content success:** Netflix's investment in original content has paid off, with the company producing numerous critically acclaimed and popular shows and movies, such as *Stranger Things*, *The Crown*, and *Squid Game*. This success has not only driven subscriber growth but also helped establish it as an acclaimed producer in the entertainment industry.

Discussion Questions:

1. How did Netflix's strategic vision and leadership contribute to its successful transition from DVD rentals to streaming services?

2. What role did technological innovation play in Netflix's ability to embrace change and capitalize on the streaming revolution?

3. How has Netflix's content strategy evolved as the company shifted its focus to streaming services, and what impact has this had on its success?

4. How did Netflix's adaptive pricing and subscription model facilitate the transition to streaming services and cater to the changing needs of its customer base?

5. In what ways can other organizations facing industry disruption learn from Netflix's approach to embracing change and adapting to new market realities?

Case Study 2: Envision the Future

Tesla's Vision for Sustainable Transportation

Overview: Tesla's groundbreaking vision for sustainable transportation has not only revolutionized the automotive industry but also inspired other companies to take bold steps in addressing environmental concerns. In this case study, we explore the background, solutions, and results of Tesla's unwavering commitment to its ambitious vision, providing valuable insights for organizations aspiring to make a difference.

Background: When Tesla formed in 2003, electric vehicles (EVs) were largely considered impractical and unfeasible due to high costs, limited range, and a scarce charging infrastructure. The automotive industry was heavily invested in internal combustion engines (ICE), and the idea of a mass-market EV seemed like a distant dream. However, Tesla's founders, led by Elon Musk in 2004, envisioned a future where EVs would be the norm, helping to reduce greenhouse gas emissions and combat climate change.

Solutions:

1. **Technology and innovation:** Tesla invested heavily in R&D to develop cutting-edge technologies that would make EVs more viable and attractive to consumers. This included innovations in battery technology, powertrain systems, and charging infrastructure—allowing Tesla to create vehicles with extended range, faster charging times, and improved performance compared to existing EVs (or hybrids and ICE vehicles).

2. **Product roadmap:** The company devised a strategic product roadmap to make its vision a reality. It started with the high-end Roadster in 2008 (to gain cash and industry recognition) and gradually moved toward more affordable, mass-market vehicles like the Model 3 and Model Y. This visionary approach allowed the company to build brand credibility and generate revenue to fund further development and expansion.

3. **Vertical integration:** Tesla took a vertically integrated approach to its supply chain and manufacturing processes, enabling the company to have greater control over produc-

tion costs, quality, and timelines. It also allowed Tesla to scale production more effectively and respond to market demands faster.

4. **Building a charging station network:** Recognizing the importance of a robust charging infrastructure for EV adoption, Tesla invested in the development of its Supercharger network. This global network of fast-charging stations has played a crucial role in alleviating range anxiety for Tesla owners and promoted the widespread adoption of EVs.

Results:

1. **Market leadership:** Tesla's unwavering commitment to its vision has resulted in the company becoming the undisputed leader in the EV market, achieving a significant share of global EV sales.

2. **Industry transformation:** The company's success has spurred the entire automotive industry to invest in EV technology. Many traditional (ICE) automakers have plans to transition to electric or hybrid vehicles—and most are doing so now.

3. **Environmental impact:** The widespread adoption of Tesla's vehicles and the subsequent increase in EVs from other automakers have contributed to a reduction in greenhouse gas emissions and to a move toward more sustainable transportation.

Discussion Questions:

1. How have Tesla's technology and innovation efforts helped the company achieve its vision for sustainable transportation?

2. In what ways has Tesla's strategic product roadmap enabled the company to overcome initial skepticism and market barriers?

3. How has Tesla's vertically integrated approach to supply chain and manufacturing contributed to its success in the EV market?

4. What role has Tesla's Supercharger network played in promoting the adoption of EVs and furthering the company's vision for sustainable transportation?

5. How can other organizations use Tesla's example to develop and execute their own bold visions for a better future?

Case Study 3: Empower Leadership Team

Google's Culture of Collaboration and Innovation

Overview: Google's journey from a small start-up to one of the world's most influential technology companies (and brands) offers valuable lessons on the power of an empowered leadership team. It highlights the importance of fostering a culture of collaboration and innovation. In this exploration of Google's approach to leadership, we delve deeper into the background, solutions, and results that've made the company a global powerhouse.

Background: When Google was established in 1998, the internet landscape was still in its infancy—fragmented, relatively small, and disorganized. The company's founders, Larry Page and Sergey Brin, envisioned a search engine that would make information universally (and quickly) accessible and useful. As Google expanded beyond search into areas like advertising, email, mobile devices, and more, it became crucial for the company to maintain its innovative spirit and collaborative culture to continue driving growth and success.

Solutions:

1. **Flat organizational structure:** Google adopted a flat organizational structure that minimized bureaucracy and encouraged open communication between team members at all levels. This approach facilitated the flow of ideas and fostered a culture where employees felt empowered to contribute to the company's strategic direction.

2. **Psychological safety:** Its leadership team emphasized (and created) an environment where employees felt comfortable expressing their ideas and taking risks without fear of negative consequences. This sense of psychological safety enabled team members to collaborate more effectively and innovate more rapidly.

3. **Focus on talent:** Google's leadership team prioritized attracting and retaining top talent. They recognized that a diverse and talented workforce would be essential for driving innovation, and so they invested in hiring the best and brightest. By doing so, the company created a competitive and merit-based culture that rewarded innovation and performance.

4. **Data-driven decision making:** Its leaders cultivated a data-driven culture where decisions were made based on evidence and analysis rather than intuition or personal bias, ensuring the most effective allocation of resources and the pursuit of the most promising ideas.

5. **Encouraging employee autonomy:** Google empowered its employees by granting them considerable autonomy in their work and providing them with the tools and resources to explore their interests and passions. This approach led to numerous innovations, as employees felt motivated and inspired to contribute to the company's success.

Results:

1. **Groundbreaking products and services:** Google's empowered leadership team and culture of innovation have resulted in a range of groundbreaking products and services, such as Google Search, Gmail, Google Maps, Android, and more. These innovations have transformed the digital landscape and touched the lives of billions around the world.

2. **Sustained growth and success:** The company's commitment to fostering an innovative culture has allowed it to maintain its competitive edge and achieve sustained growth, even as it's evolved into a global technology giant.

3. **Attracting top talent:** Google's reputation for innovation and collaboration has made it a highly attractive employer for top talent, which enables the company to continue pushing the boundaries of technology and driving positive change.

Discussion Questions:

1. How has Google's flat organizational structure contributed to its culture of collaboration and innovation?

2. In what ways has psychological safety played a role in fostering a more innovative and collaborative environment at Google?

3. How has Google's focus on talent helped the company maintain its innovative edge as it's grown?

4. What role has data-driven decision making played in Google's success and ability to innovate?

5. How can other organizations implement similar approaches to leadership and culture to foster innovation and drive success?

Case Study 4: Explore External Context

Amazon's Expansion into New Markets

Overview: As Amazon continues to successfully expand into new markets, its ability to adapt to changing external contexts has been crucial. This case study investigates the background, solutions, and results that've driven the company's growth and allowed it to become a global leader in e-commerce and technology.

Background: Amazon's journey began in 1994 as an online bookstore. However, founder Jeff Bezos envisioned a much larger and broader future for the company. His vision was "the everything store." This ambitious goal necessitated a deep understanding of various markets and industries, as well as an ability to adapt and innovate in response to changing customer needs and competitive landscapes.

Solutions:

1. **Market research and analysis:** Amazon invested heavily in market research and analysis to understand the unique characteristics, opportunities, and challenges of each new market it entered. This information informed the company's strategies and tactics, allowing it to tailor its approach to the specific needs of each market.

2. **Continuous innovation:** Now expanded into new markets, it recognized the need for continuous innovation to stay ahead of the competition. The company fostered a culture of experimentation, encouraging employees to take risks and learn from failures. This allowed Amazon to

quickly develop new products, services, and technologies that catered to the evolving needs of its customers.

3. **Learning from competitors:** Amazon has been adept at learning from its competitors and adapting its strategies accordingly. By analyzing the successes and failures of other companies, it's been able to refine its approach and identify opportunities for growth.

4. **Building strategic partnerships:** The company has leveraged strategic partnerships and alliances to accelerate its expansion into new markets. These partnerships have enabled Amazon to access new customers, distribution channels, and technologies, giving it a competitive advantage in the marketplace.

5. **Agile decision-making:** Amazon's leadership team has embraced an agile decision-making process, which has allowed the company to quickly respond to changes in the external environment. By maintaining a flexible approach, it's been able to seize opportunities and address challenges more effectively than its competitors.

Results:

1. **Diversified business portfolio:** Amazon's ability to explore the external context has allowed the company to diversify its business portfolio so that it doesn't have to rely on any single market or industry. This diversification has helped insulate the company from economic downturns and industry-specific risks.

2. **Global market leadership:** The company's expansion into new markets has enabled it to become a global leader in e-commerce, cloud computing, and other technology sectors. Amazon's success in these areas has driven significant growth in its revenues and market capitalization.

3. **Customer loyalty and trust:** By focusing on and understanding the unique needs of customers in each market, Amazon has been able to develop products and services that resonate with consumers. This customer-centric approach has fostered loyalty and trust, which further fuels the company's growth.

Discussion Questions:

1. How has Amazon's market research and analysis informed its strategies for entering new markets?

2. In what ways has continuous innovation helped Amazon stay ahead of the competition as it expands into new markets?

3. How has Amazon's ability to learn from competitors shaped its approach to exploring external contexts?

4. What role have strategic partnerships played in Amazon's expansion into new markets, and how can other organizations leverage partnerships in a similar manner?

5. How has agile decision making contributed to Amazon's success in adapting to changing external contexts?

Case Study 5: Examine Internal Capabilities

Apple's Culture of Innovation and Continuous Improvement

Overview: Apple's ability to harness its internal capabilities has been a key factor in its success as a technology leader. This case study highlights the background, solutions, and results that've driven the company's growth and allowed it to remain at the forefront of its industry.

Background: Apple's beginnings in a small garage in the late 1970s laid the foundation for its culture of innovation and continuous improvement. As the company grew, it faced increasing competition and rapidly changing market conditions but maintained that "garage" creativity and innovation. It remained focused on extracting internal capabilities to maintain its competitive edge.

Solutions:

1. **Talent acquisition and retention:** Apple prioritized hiring and keeping top talent. It created an environment where skilled employees could collaborate, innovate, and excel, and it offered competitive compensation packages while cultivating a strong corporate culture to attract and retain the best in the industry.

2. **Cross-functional collaboration:** The company encouraged collaboration across different functions and departments, fostering an environment where ideas and knowledge are shared freely. This collaborative approach allowed Apple to identify and exploit synergies between varied areas of expertise, resulting in more innovative and cohesive products.

3. **Commitment to excellence:** Apple's leadership team set high expectations for product quality, design, and performance. This excellence paradigm permeated the organization, enticing employees to continually improve their work and strive for perfection.

4. **Emphasis on design:** The company recognized the importance of design to differentiate its products and create a unique customer experience. It invested heavily in its design team and gave it the autonomy and resources needed to develop the groundbreaking artistry that's come to define the Apple brand.

5. **Strategic investments:** Apple made strategic investments in research and development (R&D), supply chain optimization, and manufacturing capabilities, which allowed the company to maintain a competitive advantage. Also, it developed new technologies and products more efficiently than its competitors.

Results:

1. **Industry-defining products:** Apple's ability to extract internal capabilities has resulted in a plethora of groundbreaking products, such as the iPod, iPhone, iPad, and Apple Watch. These products have not only generated significant revenue for the company but have also reshaped entire industries.

2. **Strong brand loyalty:** The company's commitment to innovation and continuous improvement has fostered strong brand loyalty among customers. This has been a key driver of Apple's growth, allowing it to charge premium prices for top-notch products.

3. **Market leadership:** Apple's ability to harness its internal capabilities has solidified its position as a market leader in various technology sectors, including computers, smartphones, tablets, and wearables. This market leadership has translated into significant financial success for the company.

Discussion Questions:

1. How has Apple's focus on talent acquisition and retention contributed to its innovative culture and success as a company?

2. In what ways has cross-functional collaboration within Apple led to more innovative and cohesive products?

3. How has Apple's commitment to excellence influenced its approach to product development and overall business strategy?

4. What role has Apple's emphasis on design played in its ability to differentiate its products and create a unique customer experience?

5. How have Apple's strategic investments in R&D, supply chain optimization, and manufacturing capabilities allowed the company to maintain a competitive advantage, as well as develop new technologies and products more efficiently than its competitors?

Case Study 6: Establish Resource Allocation

Microsoft's Strategic Shift to Cloud Computing

Overview: Microsoft's strategic shift to cloud computing serves as an exemplary illustration of how effective resource allocation can drive success in emerging markets. Delving deeper into the background, solutions, and results, this case study explores how Microsoft balanced investments, navigated challenges, and, ultimately, transformed its business to become a major player in the cloud-computing market.

Background: The rapid rise of cloud computing in the early 2000s caught the attention of Microsoft, which had been primarily focused on its traditional software ventures, such as MS Windows and MS Office. But the company soon recognized that embracing cloud computing was crucial to its long-term success and that it needed to effectively allocate resources to compete in this exciting new market. The transition was not without its challenges. Microsoft had to strike a balance between investing in cloud computing and maintaining its existing (and highly profitable) ventures.

Solutions:

1. **Prioritization of cloud initiatives:** Microsoft identified cloud computing as a strategic priority. It dedicated significant resources to developing its cloud services, such as Azure. This enabled it to accelerate its entry into the cloud market and eventually establish itself as a major player.

2. **Incremental investments:** The company adopted a phased approach to resource allocation. It made incremental investments in cloud computing while maintaining support for its traditional areas of focus, which allowed the company to minimize risks associated with a sudden strategic shift and enabled it to learn and adapt as the cloud market evolved.

3. **Talent development and acquisition:** It invested in talent development and acquisition to build a workforce with the necessary skills and expertise to succeed in the cloud-computing market. The company also provided training and development programs for its existing employees while recruiting top outside talent.

4. **Partner ecosystem:** Microsoft cultivated a robust partner ecosystem to support its cloud-computing initiatives. The company worked closely with a wide range of partners, from software vendors to systems integrators, to offer customers comprehensive cloud solutions and drive adoption of its cloud services.

5. **Innovation and R&D:** It continued to invest heavily in research and development while seeking new opportunities and technologies to advance its cloud-computing capabilities. This commitment to innovation enabled the company to remain at the forefront of the rapidly evolving cloud market.

Results:

1. **Rapid growth in cloud market:** Microsoft's strategic resource allocation has enabled it to achieve rapid growth in the cloud-computing market. The company's cloud services, such as Azure, have seen significant revenue growth, making it now one of the top players in the market.

2. **Diversified revenue streams:** The successful expansion into cloud computing has allowed Microsoft to diversify its revenue streams and reduce its reliance on traditional software products, as well as increase its resilience in the face of changing market conditions.

3. **Improved competitiveness:** Microsoft's strong presence in the cloud-computing market has enhanced its overall competitiveness, positioning the company for continued success in the technology industry.

Discussion Questions:

1. How has Microsoft's prioritization of cloud initiatives impacted its ability to compete in the cloud-computing market?

2. In what ways has Microsoft's incremental approach to resource allocation helped it manage risks associated with a strategic shift?

3. How has talent development and acquisition contributed to Microsoft's success in cloud computing?

4. What role has Microsoft's partner ecosystem played in driving the adoption of its cloud services?

5. How has Microsoft's commitment to innovation and R&D helped the company maintain its competitiveness in the rapidly evolving cloud market?

Case Study 7: Execute Strategic Action

Airbnb's Expansion and Growth Strategy

Overview: Airbnb's remarkable expansion and growth strategy serve as a powerful paradigm for organizations seeking to execute its strategic plans effectively. In this case study, we delve deeper into the background, solutions, and results of Airbnb's successful growth strategy, highlighting how the company tackled challenges, implemented initiatives, and almost single-handedly disrupted the travel and hospitality industry.

Background: Airbnb's meteoric rise as a home-sharing platform rattled the traditional lodging sector, but the company knew that it needed to execute a well-thought-out strategic plan to continue its growth trajectory. It needed to address challenges such as regulatory hurdles, competition from traditional lodging providers, and the ever-evolving demands of users. Its goal was not just to expand its services but also to create a sustainable business model that would continue to drive long-term success.

Solutions:

1. **Comprehensive change roadmap:** Airbnb developed a detailed change roadmap to guide its expansion and growth strategy. It entailed entering new markets, broadening offerings, and forming strategic partnerships with local governments and industry stakeholders. The roadmap provided a clear direction for the company and helped align the organization's efforts around shared goals.

2. **Agile project management:** Recognizing the need for adaptability in a rapidly changing industry, Airbnb adopted an agile project management approach, allowing it to quickly respond to changes in the market, adapt its strategic initiatives as needed, and continue moving forward with its growth strategy.

3. **Clear communication:** Airbnb understood the importance of clear communication when executing a strategic plan. It maintained open channels of communication among team members and stakeholders, ensuring that everyone was aligned with the organization's goals and aware of their role in achieving them.

4. **Regular performance reviews:** To monitor the progress of its strategic plan, Airbnb conducted regular performance reviews, which provided valuable insights into the effectiveness of its initiatives, identified areas for improvement, and made data-driven decisions to support its growth strategy.

5. **Continuous learning and improvement:** Airbnb fostered a culture of continuous learning and improvement, encouraging team members to learn from both successes and setbacks. This approach helped the company refine its strategic plan and maintain momentum on its growth journey.

Results:

1. **Expanded services:** As a result of the successful execution of its strategic plan, Airbnb expanded its services to include experiences and boutique hotels, broadening its appeal to a wider range of travelers.

2. **Increased user base:** Its growth initiatives have led to a significant increase in its user base, establishing the company as a major player in the travel and hospitality industry.

3. **Global presence:** The company's strategic plan enabled it to enter new markets and establish a strong global presence, which further solidified its position in the industry.

4. **Enhanced brand reputation:** Airbnb's successful execution of its strategic plan has contributed to an enhanced

brand reputation and made it a preferred choice for travelers seeking unique and authentic accommodations.

5. **Industry disruption:** Airbnb's growth and expansion have disrupted the traditional travel and hospitality industry, which has forced established players to adapt and rethink their business models.

Discussion Questions:

1. How has Airbnb's comprehensive change roadmap contributed to the successful execution of its strategic plan?

2. What role has agile project management played in Airbnb's ability to adapt to changing market conditions?

3. How has clear communication contributed to the alignment of team members and stakeholders around Airbnb's strategic goals?

4. In what ways have regular performance reviews and continuous learning and improvement helped Airbnb refine its strategic plan and maintain momentum?

5. How has Airbnb's successful execution of its strategic plan disrupted the traditional travel and hospitality industry, and what implications does this have for the future of the sector?

Case Study 8: Encourage the Heart

Southwest Airlines' Employee-Centric Culture

Overview: Southwest Airlines' commitment to an employee-centric culture has been crucial to its resilience and success in the airline industry. In this case study, we delve deeper into the background, solutions, and results of Southwest's culture and how it encourages the heart, as well as how it's helped the company achieve exceptional business outcomes. The commitment to its team isn't just reflected in the company's mission statement but is deeply ingrained in its daily operations. The company acknowledges that its employees are its most valuable assets, with their happiness directly influencing the quality of service delivered to its customers.

Background: Southwest Airlines, a leading U.S. airline, has long been celebrated for its unique, employee-centric culture. The company believes that by creating an engaging and positive work environment, it can foster employee satisfaction, which, in turn, leads to higher customer satisfaction and business success. However, maintaining this culture isn't without its challenges, particularly in an industry known for its volatility, stringent regulations, and intense competition. But Southwest has shown great resilience and navigated several industry downturns, fluctuating fuel costs, labor disputes, and the need for constant innovation to stay competitive.

Solutions:

1. **Communication:** Southwest's leadership has prioritized transparency and open dialogue, ensuring that employees are well informed and feel valued. Regular town-hall-style meetings and an open-door policy foster a sense of inclusivity and trust.

2. **Recognition:** The airline has established programs to acknowledge and reward employees' hard work and dedication, such as the "Winning Spirit Award," which recognizes those who go above and beyond in their service.

3. **Celebration:** Southwest is known for celebrating its milestones and successes, which helps boost morale and cultivate a sense of shared achievement.

4. **Training and development:** To equip employees with the necessary skills and knowledge, Southwest invests in ongoing training and development programs.

5. **Employee benefits:** Generous benefits, including profit-sharing and free air travel, further demonstrate the company's commitment to its employees.

Results:

1. **Employee satisfaction:** Southwest's employee-centric practices have resulted in high employee satisfaction rates, which, in turn, positively impacts customer satisfaction.

2. **Reputation:** The airline is consistently ranked as one of the best places to work, attracting and retaining top talent in the industry.

3. **Customer satisfaction:** With a happy and engaged workforce, Southwest has maintained high levels of customer satisfaction despite the industry's challenges.

4. **Resilience:** The strong culture has helped Southwest navigate industry downturns more effectively than many of its competitors.

5. **Profitability:** The company's approach has translated into financial success, with Southwest remaining profitable for 47 consecutive years—a record unmatched in the U.S. airline industry.

Discussion Questions:

1. What aspects of Southwest's culture have contributed to its high levels of employee and customer satisfaction?

2. How have Southwest's recognition and reward programs impacted employee engagement and performance?

3. How has Southwest maintained its employee-centric culture despite the challenges inherent in the airline industry?

4. What role has the celebration of milestones and successes played in Southwest's ability to foster a sense of shared achievement and camaraderie among employees?

5. What can other organizations learn from Southwest's approach to encouraging the heart, particularly in industries that are highly competitive or volatile?

Case Study 9: Evaluate Results

Spotify's Data-Driven Approach to Improve User Experience

Overview: Spotify's relentless commitment to evaluating results and using data to drive continuous improvement is a crucial factor behind its success in the music streaming industry. In this case study, we explore the background, solutions, and results of Spotify's data-driven approach to improving user experience. We offer insights into how the company measures the impact of its efforts and uses data to inform its product development and improvement strategies.

Background: As a leading music streaming service, Spotify knew that it needed to consistently evaluate and enhance its user experience to maintain a competitive edge, but it faced the challenge of quantifying the impact of its efforts. To this end, it ensured that its product development and improvement strategies were data-driven and effective. The company established clear success metrics and indicators, implemented regular performance reviews, and utilized user feedback to inform its decisions.

Solutions:

1. **Clear success metrics and indicators:** Spotify established specific success metrics and indicators, such as user engagement and retention, to evaluate its performance. By focusing on these key metrics, the company could measure the effectiveness of its efforts and identify areas for improvement.

2. **Regular performance reviews:** The company implemented regular performance reviews to track its progress against its success metrics and indicators. These reviews provided valuable insights into the impact of its efforts and enabled the company to make data-driven decisions to enhance its user experience.

3. **Feedback loops:** Spotify recognized the importance of user feedback in informing its product development and improvement strategies, and so it used various channels to collect user feedback, such as surveys and in-app ratings. It incorporated this feedback into its decision-making process.

4. **Data-driven approach:** The company adopted a data-driven approach to evaluating results, and it utilized data analytics and machine learning to gain insights into user behavior and preferences. This approach allowed Spotify to identify trends and patterns, informing its product development and improvement strategies and continually enhancing the user experience.

5. **Continuous improvement culture:** Spotify cultivated a culture of continuous improvement. It encouraged team members to learn from both successes and setbacks, which helped the company maintain its focus on evaluating results and driving ongoing improvements to its user experience.

Results:

1. **Enhanced user experience:** Spotify's data-driven approach to evaluating results has allowed the company to continually improve its user experience by offering personalized recommendations, curated playlists, and seamless integration across devices.

2. **Increased user engagement:** As a result of its focus on evaluating results and enhancing user experience, Spotify has seen increased user engagement. Accordingly, users spend more time listening to music and interacting with the platform.

3. **User retention:** By continually evaluating and improving its user experience, Spotify has been able to retain users and keep them coming back for more, which has contributed to the company's overall growth and success.

4. **Competitive edge:** The company's relentless commitment to evaluating results and using data to drive continuous improvement has helped it to maintain its competitive edge in the music streaming industry, differentiating it from its competitors.

5. **Growth and success:** Spotify's focus on evaluating results and improving user experience has played a significant role in the company's growth and success, establishing it as a dominant player in the music streaming market.

Discussion Questions:

1. How has Spotify's establishment of clear success metrics and indicators contributed to its data-driven approach to evaluating results?

2. What role have regular performance reviews and feedback loops played in Spotify's continuous improvement efforts?

3. How has Spotify's data-driven approach to evaluating results informed its product development and improvement strategies?

4. In what ways has the culture of continuous improvement at Spotify contributed to the company's ability to maintain its competitive edge in the music streaming industry?

5. What are the long-term implications of Spotify's focus on evaluating results and improving user experience for its growth and success in the market?

Case Study 10: Evolutionary Process

Zappos' Emphasis on Company Culture and Adaptability

Overview: Zappos, the online shoe retailer, recognized the importance of fostering a culture of continuous learning and adaptation, giving it, fittingly, a leg up in the highly competitive online retail industry. This case study delves into the background, solutions, and results of Zappos' emphasis on company culture and adaptability—and sheds some light on how the company has remained a leader in the industry while successfully navigating shifting market dynamics.

Background: Zappos needed to sustain its growth and momentum amid increasing competition and changing consumer preferences. The company faced the challenge of fostering a culture of continuous learning and adaptation to stay ahead of the curve. To do this, Zappos prioritized creating a culture that embraced change and innovation, preparing it for future disruptions and opportunities.

Solutions:

1. **Culture of continuous learning:** Zappos prioritized creating a culture of continuous learning and adaptation. It

recognized that change and innovation are vital for long-term success, and so it offered ongoing training and development programs for employees, encouraging them to learn new skills and embrace change.

2. **Encouraging experimentation and risk taking:** It also created an environment where employees were encouraged to take risks, experiment with new ideas, and learn from failure. This approach helped the company uncover new opportunities and stay ahead of emerging trends and technologies.

3. **Embedding change and innovation:** Zappos embedded change and innovation into its organizational DNA, ensuring that adaptability became a core part of its identity. This commitment to embracing change helped the company remain agile and responsive to shifting market dynamics.

4. **Employee empowerment:** The company empowered its employees by giving them the autonomy and resources needed to drive change and innovation, which fostered a sense of ownership and accountability among team members by encouraging them to contribute to the company's growth and success.

5. **Maintaining a strong company culture:** Zappos placed a strong emphasis on its company culture, believing that a positive and supportive work environment would inspire employees to embrace change and contribute to its long-term success. The company's core values and unique culture have been widely recognized and celebrated.

Results:

1. **Industry leadership:** Zappos' emphasis on company culture and adaptability has allowed it to remain a leader in

the online retail industry—and helped it maintain a competitive edge and attract a loyal customer base.

2. **Adaptability:** Its focus on continuous learning and adaptation has enabled Zappos to navigate shifting market dynamics, effectively responding to changes in consumer preferences, emerging technologies, and competitive threats.

3. **Innovation:** The company's commitment to fostering a culture of change and innovation has led to the development of new products, services, and business models, ensuring that it remains at the forefront of the online retail industry.

4. **Employee engagement:** Zappos' focus on employee development and empowerment has resulted in a highly engaged and motivated workforce, with employees committed to driving change and innovation within the company.

5. **Growth and success:** The emphasis on continuous learning and adaptation has positively impacted Zappos' growth and success, enabling it to expand product offerings and market reach.

Discussion Questions:

1. How has Zappos' focus on employee development and empowerment contributed to its culture of continuous learning and adaptation?

2. What role has Zappos' unique company culture played in fostering a culture of change and innovation?

3. How has Zappos' commitment to embracing change and innovation enabled the company to navigate shifting market dynamics and maintain its competitive edge?

4. What lessons can other organizations learn from Zappos' approach to sustaining change and momentum through a culture of continuous learning and adaptation?

5. How might Zappos' focus on company culture and adaptability continue to shape the company's future growth and success?

Organizational Audit

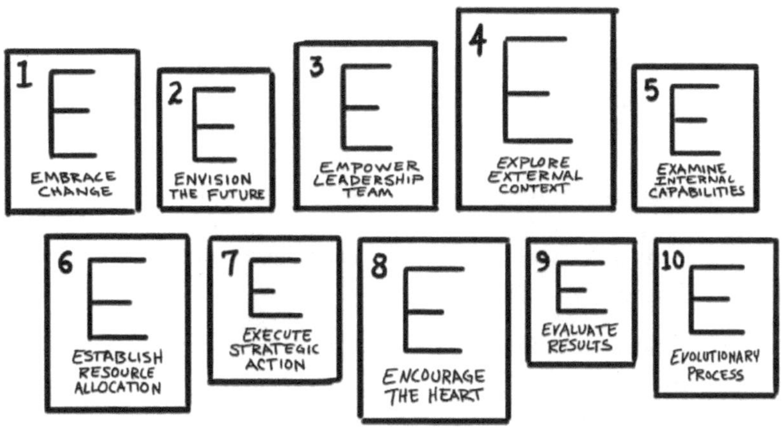

The purpose of this organizational audit is to assess a company's readiness and capabilities in executing strategic change, innovation, and transformation. Based on the 10 Elements of Successful Change Leadership, this audit helps identify strengths, weaknesses, opportunities, and threats within an organization.

The 10 Elements of Successful Change Leadership

1. **Embrace Change: Cultivating a Growth Mindset**

- Assess the organization's mindset toward change, learning, and adaptability.

- Evaluate the level of openness to new ideas and approaches among leadership and employees.

- Identify initiatives and practices that support the development of a growth mindset within the organization.

2. **Envision the Future: Charting a Bold Course**

- Analyze the company's vision for the future, including long-term goals and strategic direction.

- Assess the clarity and alignment of the vision with the organization's mission and values.

- Evaluate the communication of the vision to employees and stakeholders, as well as their level of engagement.

3. **Empower the Leadership Team: Assembling a Cohesive Force**

- Assess the composition, diversity, and complementary skills of the leadership team.

- Evaluate the leadership team's effectiveness in fostering a culture of collaboration, innovation, and shared accountability.

- Analyze the team's ability to make decisions, delegate authority, and empower employees.

4. **Explore External Context: Deciphering the Business Landscape**

- Examine the organization's understanding of its market, competitors, and external forces shaping the industry.

- Assess the company's ability to identify opportunities, threats, and emerging trends.

- Evaluate the organization's use of partnerships, alliances, and collaborations to gain a competitive advantage.

5. **Examine Internal Capabilities: Unearthing Hidden Potential**

- Analyze the organization's strengths and weaknesses, including core competencies, resources, and assets.

- Assess the company's ability to leverage its internal capabilities for strategic advantage.

- Evaluate the organization's efforts to continuously improve and innovate its products, services, and processes.

6. **Establish Resource Allocation: Fueling the Engine of Change**

- Assess the organization's strategic allocation of financial, human, and technological resources.

- Evaluate the balance between short-term and long-term investments to ensure agility and flexibility in resource allocation.

- Analyze the company's ability to prioritize and align resources with strategic priorities.

7. **Execute Strategic Action: Translating Vision into an Action Plan**

- Examine the organization's strategic planning process, including the development of clear objectives, milestones, and performance indicators.

- Assess the company's project management capabilities, communication, and coordination across teams.

- Evaluate the effectiveness of monitoring and reviewing progress toward strategic goals.

8. **Encourage the Heart: Igniting Passion and Commitment**

- Analyze the organization's efforts to inspire and motivate employees through recognition, rewards, and support.

- Assess the company's ability to create a sense of purpose and belonging among its employees.
- Evaluate the impact of leadership behavior on employee engagement, commitment, and morale.

9. Evaluate Results: Assessing the Impact of Change

- Examine the organization's use of data, metrics, and indicators to measure the success of its change initiatives.
- Assess the company's ability to learn from successes and failures and apply insights to future initiatives.
- Evaluate the effectiveness of feedback loops, performance reviews, and continuous improvement processes.

10. Evolutionary Process: Sustaining Change and Momentum

- Analyze the organization's capacity to maintain and sustain change efforts over time.
- Assess the company's ability to anticipate and prepare for future disruptions and opportunities.
- Evaluate the organization's practices and policies for fostering a culture of continuous learning, adaptation, and innovation.

Leading Strategic Change Course

This ten-week curriculum (based on my 10 Elements of Successful Change Leadership) provides a comprehensive exploration of change leadership, innovation, and organizational transformation. Throughout the course, participants engage in a variety of group activities, breakout sessions, team discussions, and homework and journaling exercises—all designed to deepen your understanding of the core concepts and principles of successful change leadership.

Each week, a different module covers a specific element of change leadership, including creating a compelling vision, fostering a collaborative culture, exploring external contexts, leveraging internal capabilities, executing strategic plans, and evaluating results. We examine the importance of adaptability, continuous learning, and social and environmental responsibility. Real-world case studies from leading companies, such as Apple, Tesla, Google, and Southwest Airlines, are integrated into the program to provide practical examples and demonstrate the relevance of the concepts being discussed.

By the end of the ten-week leadership course, emerging leaders gain valuable insights and practical skills to lead their organizations more effectively and navigate the challenges of today's dynamic business landscape. The curriculum (outlined below) equips future leaders with the tools and strategies necessary for fostering innovation, driving transformation, and achieving long-term success in their respective fields.

Week 1: Embrace Change

- Introduction to change leadership and its importance in today's business environment
- Discuss the concept of embracing change and its impact on organizational success

- In-class group activity: Case study analysis ("Netflix's Shift from DVD Rentals to Streaming")

- Breakout session: Share personal experiences of embracing change within organizations

- Class discussion: Key factors that contribute to successful change

- Homework and journaling: Reflect on personal strengths and weaknesses in embracing change

Week 2: Envision the Future

- Explore the importance of envisioning the future and setting goals

- Discuss the role of visionary leadership in driving innovation and transformation

- In-class group activity: Case study analysis ("Tesla's Vision for Sustainable Transportation")

- Breakout session: Brainstorm ideas for future goals within participants' organizations

- Class discussion: Obstacles in envisioning and achieving future goals

- Homework and journaling: Create a personal vision statement and set goals for the next three years

Week 3: Empower Leadership Team

- Examine the significance of a strong and empowered leadership team

- Discuss strategies for fostering collaboration, trust, and innovation within leadership teams

- In-class group activity: Case study analysis ("Google's Culture of Collaboration and Innovation")

- Breakout session: Develop a plan for empowering leadership within participants' organizations

- Class discussion: Challenges and best practices in creating empowered leadership teams

- Homework and journaling: Reflect on personal leadership style and areas for improvement

Week 4: Explore External Context

- Understand the importance of assessing external context when entering new markets

- Discuss strategies for conducting market analysis and identifying opportunities and threats

- In-class group activity: Case study analysis ("Amazon's Expansion into New Markets")

- Breakout session: Conduct a SWOT analysis for a potential market entry

- Class discussion: The role of external partnerships and alliances in exploring new markets

- Homework and journaling: Identify an emerging market or trend and discuss potential opportunities

Week 5: Examine Internal Capabilities

- Learn how to assess and leverage organizational strengths and weaknesses

- Discuss the importance of a culture of innovation and continuous improvement

- In-class group activity: Case study analysis ("Apple's Culture of Innovation and Continuous Improvement")

- Breakout session: Identify internal capabilities within participants' organizations and potential areas for improvement

- Class discussion: Strategies for fostering a culture of innovation
- Homework and journaling: Reflect on personal strengths and areas for improvement within the workplace

Week 6: Establish Resource Allocation

- Explore the importance of strategic resource allocation in driving organizational growth
- Discuss strategies for balancing short-term and long-term investments
- In-class group activity: Case study analysis ("Microsoft's Strategic Shift to Cloud Computing")
- Breakout session: Develop a resource-allocation plan for a strategic initiative within participants' organizations
- Class discussion: Challenges and best practices in resource allocation
- Homework and journaling: Evaluate personal time and resource management skills

Week 7: Execute Strategic Action

- Understand the importance of executing a strategic plan for growth and expansion
- Discuss strategies for effective communication, agile project management, and performance reviews
- In-class group activity: Case study analysis ("Airbnb's Expansion and Growth Strategy")
- Breakout session: Create a change roadmap for a strategic initiative within participants' organizations
- Class discussion: The role of organizational culture in executing strategic plans

- Homework and journaling: Assess personal effectiveness in executing plans and setting goals

Week 8: Encourage the Heart

- Understand the role of emotional investment and intrinsic motivation in driving change and transformation

- Discuss strategies for fostering an environment that values, recognizes, and rewards employee contributions

- In-class group activity: Case study analysis ("Southwest Airlines' Employee-Centric Culture")

- Breakout session: Develop a strategic plan for encouraging the heart within participants' organizations, focusing on recognition and reward systems, celebration of milestones, and communication of vision and values

- Class discussion: The impact of an employee-centric culture on organizational performance and the challenges of maintaining such a culture in the face of growth and industry pressures

- Homework and journaling: Reflect on personal experiences of feeling valued and recognized in a work setting, and how these experiences influenced commitment and performance

Week 9: Evaluate Results

- Examine the importance of evaluating results and driving continuous improvement

- Discuss strategies for establishing clear success metrics and indicators

- In-class group activity: Case study analysis ("Spotify's Data-Driven Approach to Improving User Experience")

- Breakout session: Develop a set of success metrics and indicators for a project within participants' organizations

- Class discussion: The role of data and user feedback in driving continuous improvement

- Homework and journaling: Reflect on personal experiences in evaluating results and adapting strategies

Week 10: Evolutionary Process

- Learn about the importance of fostering a culture of continuous learning and adaptation

- Discuss strategies for embedding change and innovation into an organization's DNA

- In-class group activity: Case study analysis ("Zappos' Emphasis on Company Culture and Adaptability")

- Breakout session: Identify ways to enhance a culture of continuous learning within participants' organizations

- Class discussion: The role of employee development and risk taking in driving organizational evolution

- Homework and journaling: Reflect on personal adaptability and openness to change

About The Author

Dr. Christopher P. Meade holds a PhD in Adult & Organizational Learning with a concentration in leadership from the University of Idaho. He also holds two master's degrees and a certificate in Disruptive Strategy from Harvard Business School. A former business school dean and acclaimed graduate instructor, Christopher has coached and trained more than 25,000 leaders and facilitated team training for numerous Fortune 500 organizations. Christopher speaks at leadership events and team training events throughout the United States. He is the author of multiple books on leadership and personal and professional development, including *Leadership Alive: Changing Leadership Practices in the Emerging 21st Century Culture; Team Accelerators: The Seven Force Multipliers of High-Performance Teams; Servantology: The Period Elements of Servant Leadership; Emotional Intelligence: Another Kind of Smart; Trust Accelerators: Activating the Domino Effect That Accelerates Team Engagement, Innovation, and High-Performance;* and *Trusted Servant Leadership: A New Kind of Leader for a New Kind of World.*

> I want to inspire leaders to be extraordinary. Everything I do is designed to catalyze growth in others and propel them toward a better version of themselves so that they can more meaningfully touch the lives of others in the work they do each day.

> — Christopher P. Meade, PhD